HOW
TO MEET
YOURSELF

(and find true happiness)

Winchester, UK
Washington, USA)

First published by O Books, 2007
O Books is an imprint of John Hunt Publishing Ltd.,
The Bothy, Deershot Lodge, Park Lane, Ropley, Hants, SO24 0BE, UK
office1@o-books.net
www.o-books.net

Distribution in:

UK and Europe
Orca Book Services
orders@orcabookservices.co.uk
Tel: 01202 665432 Fax: 01202 666219 Int. code (44)

USA and Canada
NBN
custserv@nbnbooks.com
Tel: 1 800 462 6420 Fax: 1 800 338 4550

Australia and New Zealand
Brumby Books
sales@brumbybooks.com
Tel: 61 3 9761 5535 Fax: 61 3 9761 7095

Far East (offices in Singapore, Thailand, Hong Kong, Taiwan)
Pansing Distribution Pte Ltd
kemal@pansing.com
Tel: 65 6319 9939 Fax: 65 6462 5761

South Africa
Alternative Books
altbook@peterhyde.co.za
Tel: 021 447 5300 Fax: 021 447 1430

Text copyright Dennis Waite 2007

Design: Stuart Davies

ISBN-13: 978 1 84694 041 5
ISBN-10: 1 84694 041 9

A CIP catalogue record for this book is available from the British Library.

Printed in the US by Maple Vail

HOW
TO MEET
YOURSELF
(and find true happiness)

DENNIS WAITE

BOOKS

Winchester, UK
Washington, USA

You think that your life is in a mess and wonder what it all means. You are looking for an explanation and a sense of purpose. You just want to be happy.

This is not a self-help book – who you really are does not need any help. The problem is that you have completely mistaken the nature of yourself and the world. You are confusing what is real with what is unreal. Once this confusion has been untangled, both meaning and purpose will be revealed. This book will disentangle your mind! It will explain to you what you are not so that you can understand who you really are and, ultimately, come to the realization that you are already happy now!

CONTENTS

Introduction
Mars does not exist

You want to know what you should do with your life, what things really matter, discover the answers to lots of similar, related questions. So why should you read this book? What am I claiming that you will find of value in these pages? Well, suppose that the one ambition in your life is to travel to Mars. If you are sufficiently young, intelligent, athletic and determined, you might think that this is not beyond the realms of possibility. But suppose that I could prove to you that Mars simply does not exist. You might not be very pleased to discover this but then at least you would be able to drop your obviously now unattainable goal and aim instead for something that is realistic and worthwhile. The purpose of this book is to demonstrate to you that, *whatever your particular ambition might be*, Mars does not exist.

Two fundamental questions are addressed. They are probably the two most important questions you could ever ask yourself, though many people never even give them a thought. It is possible to spend a lifetime attempting to reach satisfactory answers – and many have. Before beginning, you may find it useful to ask yourself these questions now and attempt to formulate an answer. If you acknowledge your position at the outset, you will be able better to appreciate whether your views have changed by the end of the book. Books, especially those that might be classed as self-help, often ask their readers to fill out questionnaires. You may be pleased to hear that this is not one of those. I do not want you to write pages of notes. In fact a single sentence response to each question is all that I am suggesting. My own answers at the end of the book will be single words. It will be best if you do not cheat and look now, however, or you may decide not to read any further!

The questions are simply as follows (ask them of yourself):

Who am I?

What really matters?

In order to answer these questions, this book will focus on the fundamentals of our being, the world and the relationship between them, asking about our nature, motives and actions, emotions and thoughts. It will aim to provide a more consistent, logical and practical explanation than you will find from the traditional viewpoints of Western philosophy, major religions, psychology or sociology. It will systematically address key topics such as meaning and purpose, happiness and free will, the nature of the world and self, in a way that appeals directly to your own experience and reason, answering the fundamental questions of who we are and what we ought to be doing.

1. Are we missing the point to our lives?

There are many things that we do in the course of our lives. Some of these we strive for and look forward to. A few of them we may actually achieve but, more often than not, we gain only disappointment and lack of fulfillment. Do we simply want to fill the void between birth and death or do we want to feel that there is an end to be sought, to make it all somehow worthwhile? These are questions that most of us ask, at one time or another – usually when suffering depression as the result of some significant failure – but most of the time we choose to ignore them. Most of us feel that no one can ever give us a truly satisfactory answer and, when things are going well, we simply forget about them… but they are not going to go away.

Happiness is not a cigar

You may well remember the television adverts of the late nineteen eighties and early nineties, before tobacco advertising was banned. There was a series of very clever, funny and popular commercials for a certain cigar from Benson and Hedges. They took the form of a man single-mindedly pursuing some activity, the successful outcome of which would realize some long-term ambition and bring about fulfillment, satisfaction and gratification. Just as the goal is about to be reached, there is some trivial and amusing occurrence and the achievement is prevented - the anticipation of joy is replaced by the reality of despair. Dejected, the man takes out his packet of cigars and lights one. The wistful melody from

Bach's "Air on a G String" begins. The man sinks back and a blissful smile slowly suffuses his face as the caption appears: *Happiness is a cigar called Hamlet.*

All very clever from a marketing viewpoint but, like most things in the world of advertising, it does not stand up to analysis. At best, it seems that it ought to have said "Consolation is a cigar called Hamlet." After all, smoking a cigar was never the object of the exercise and he could have done this at any time. If you want something very much and fail to get it when it is almost within grasp, it scarcely seems plausible that setting some smelly weed on fire could suddenly bring happiness.

The scenarios for these adverts were many and varied over the years. The beauty of them was that you could easily substitute your own pet desire of the moment, imagine failing to achieve it and fall into the trap of assuming that the cigar would provide solace - excellent for the shareholders of Benson and Hedges; not necessarily too brilliant for your health. The point of giving this example, however, and the purpose of this book, is to ask whether the realization of *any* of the usual ambitions can ever bring lasting happiness. What things in life *actually* matter?

There certainly are people who feel that they have discovered meaning and purpose in their own lives. Such people can almost be recognized, if you are with them for long enough, by the aura of peace and confidence that seems to surround them. They are secure in the knowledge that nothing can faze them. They have their aim in life and exercise total commitment in working towards it. You want to discover their secret so that you can share their positive attitude and presumed happiness... but then maybe you discover that they are born-again Christians and are not yourself religiously inclined.

The dinner party

At each level of our everyday lives, it seems to me that we often fail to appreciate what really matters. We concentrate disproportionate effort upon incidentals or become side-tracked into irrelevancies, sometimes to the extent that the main purpose is forgotten or overlooked. We own a car so that we can travel from A to B more conveniently/comfortably/quickly but we spend hours every week cleaning and polishing it so that it looks impressive sitting in the driveway. We spend an enormous number of hours working in our highly paid jobs so that we may be able to relax in luxury or do what we want in our spare time, only to discover that we do not have any spare time and instead contract ulcers, heart disease and divorces.

Here is a very simple example, providing that my wife will allow me to use it. Like most people, I enjoy having friends or relations round for a meal occasionally, even though I am basically an unsociable and boring person. Unfortunately, the event does not take place in isolation and what particularly irritates me is that my wife will spend days beforehand worrying about it and disturbing us both. The house has to be cleaned. The recipe books come out and are searched through again, inviting some new, previously unseen idea for a meal to leap suddenly from the page. The weekly trip to the supermarket results in innumerable extras of food not normally purchased, which we will have to eat our way through for the rest of the week after the visitors have gone. Quite possibly the day before and certainly most of the day on which the meal is scheduled, my wife will toil in the kitchen for hours on end, filling the fridge with prepared dishes and the sink with dirty ones. It wouldn't be so bad if she did this without becoming irritable and life continued around it as normal. But no, she adopts this single-minded, determined attitude. Nothing else matters and any potential problem or unrelated need is an inconvenience. It is necessary to stay out of the way or approach the kitchen very circumspectly indeed, in case some complex procedure is nearing its culmination.

Panic point is reached several hours before the ETA, when suitable attire has to be located in the wardrobe. This is a task that is bound to fail because it is a fact ascertained time and time again that "there is never anything to wear." (This is admittedly quite understandable since, whenever we go shopping, she will look at and try on many different garments but scarcely ever actually buy anything. If she ever does, it is invariably taken back unworn for a refund, several weeks later.)

When the visitors actually arrive, there is still usually a lot to be done in the kitchen and the paramount thing is to ensure they have all they could want at all times. There is little opportunity for just relaxing and enjoying their company. And when they have finally gone, there is several days' worth of crockery and cutlery to be washed up before we can fall, exhausted, into bed. (No, we don't have a dishwasher!)

It seems to me that the only point of having visitors at all must be so that they will invite you to visit them some time later in exchange. Then the only related pain will be the "what shall I wear" aspect. OK, so perhaps I am exaggerating somewhat to make the point (I have to say this!), but it does seem inescapable that what really ought to be the purpose of this exercise – the enjoyment of the visitors – is being lost amongst the rest of the related activities.

All of this is not to suggest that we can act in defiance of what we believe really matters. What is happening in the above example is simply that, to my wife, what is *really* important is that other people think well of her. Outside of the house, she must be seen to be smartly dressed, even if in a location where no one could possibly know (or care) who she is. She must be seen to be a good housewife if there are visitors, a good cook and considerate hostess if there are party guests and so on. Any actions or spoken words must be taken in the way intended and not misunderstood.

What really concerns us will invariably affect our thoughts and actions even if it does so subconsciously. Our self-esteem may be seriously affected by what we believe others think of us. And in many cases, it may be affected adversely simply by what we *think* others think about us. The more sensitive we are the more significant will be the impact.

What *really* matters?

If we ask ourselves the question "What really matters?" the answer will often depend upon the context and will undoubtedly change over the course of our lives. For the young child, everything may be insignificant except the gaining of a particular toy similar to that owned by a friend or that has grabbed her attention on the television. An older child might be afraid to go to school unless wearing a peer-approved pair of trainers. The teenager may be unable to eat or concentrate, worrying about a potential boy or girlfriend. As we grow older, there seem to be many more important things to concern us. Where is the money to come from for the mortgage repayments or even the next meal? Will I be made redundant? Will the tests at the hospital be positive? There seems to be no end to the trials that beset us and, at any given time, there will be one thing whose immediacy and potential for pain and embarrassment or happiness and fulfillment raises it above all others in importance.

Perhaps, to enable us to relegate the day to day problems and concentrate the mind, we should underline the significance and ask "What really matters?" This might allow us to look away from the selfish (and insignificant?) personal matters and towards a more general context. Surely it is more important that the Middle East issues are resolved, that the Al Qaeda terrorist groups are found and disbanded and so on. This, of course, assumes that those problems that affect many people must necessarily be of greater consequence than those that impact only me, even if the former do not affect me at all. Is this a reasonable view? Certainly the attitude that the optimal action is the one that results in the greater happiness of the majority is one that has had much influence.

But then, even if we only admit it to ourselves, it is quite likely that a more correct underlining of the question should be "What really matters *to me*?" With this slant, we are bound to turn towards such considerations as my living a long life, staying healthy, and being happy. Of course this will manifest itself in different ways according to those aspects that we consider important at the time of asking. We may, for example, want our children to have a good education, obtain well-paid jobs, have a joyful marriage etc. That is to say, we may measure our own achievement through that of our offspring as though, not having obtained these things for ourselves to our own satisfaction, we would like to think that they will. (It is, of course, unreasonable to think that we will be remembered for any achievement by our future descendants. How many people even know the *names* of their great-grandparents?)

This view is reinforced most strongly by those couples who are unable to have children for one reason or another. The sort of expression used by the would-be mother is that she is *desperate* to have children. It is as though we are running a relay race with some clear goal of achievement and, although we have not managed to pass the finishing post, those to whom we pass the baton might. And here it is the fact that they are *our* children that is important – i.e. they have our genetic inheritance and are therefore somehow a part of ourselves. If we do not have children who can take over our race, then we are certain to lose.

In the extreme, we see this in some other creatures, such as the Praying Mantis male. He happily submits to having its head bitten off by the female, secure in the knowledge that the secondary brain in its abdomen will keep intercourse going until the female is impregnated and thereby propagate his genes. This view that our purpose is evolutionary, that all of our desires and activities are directly or indirectly working towards the end of passing on our genes to another generation is one that is held by many current thinkers.

As soon as we begin to think about all of these things, it quickly becomes apparent that the subject is a difficult one. What exactly should we want/expect from life? Does it really make any difference what happens to us, or to the human race for that matter? Can we change anything so as to move from a position of dissatisfaction to one of consummation? Who am I, anyway? What is my place in the scheme of things? What, indeed, is the world and reality?

Perhaps it is the answers to these questions that really matter, at least initially. If we do not know who we are, where we are going, and whether there is ultimately any answer to any of the earlier questions, then we might be wasting our time. If, for example, we only have this life here and now, and if there is some end that should be sought, then we really ought to be doing something towards it before it is too late. Certainly if there are answers, it must make all the difference to our lives to be aware of them. Instead of losing sleep and concentration over the myriad things that we worry about, we could ignore all of the trivial ones and give our attention only to those that are important.

But which criteria should be used to determine what the important things in life are? I may accept the prompting of my parents that I need to get a good job in order to avoid many of the potential discomforts and intellectually I may know that I should be directing all my efforts to revising for the end of year exams. But if I am unable to concentrate because I cannot stop thinking about the girl I met last week, what am I to do? Is it the case that my intellect is claiming that x really matters while my emotions (or hormones) say that it is y? How should this sort of situation be resolved? My religious beliefs may point me in one direction and my scientific background in another. My teachers may advise one course and my peers something different. This book may overthrow a lifetime of learned convictions. Why should you pay any attention?

These, then, are the subjects of this book. I will endeavor to address each of the general areas that we might consider to really matter at one time or another and investigate whether they should be considered important. We will look at those things that actually seem to matter to us – bodily health, emotions such as love, intellectual pursuits, our relationship to others and society etc. – all of which we might think must ultimately carry more weight than the petty concerns of little me. We will specifically ask the questions "What is the nature of the world and reality?" and "Who am I?" and attempt to find satisfactory answers. We will examine the criteria by which we believe we make choices and ask whether we actually choose at all. Finally, we will look at what we can do to follow up on what has been discussed, to consolidate our understanding and begin to live our lives in recognition of the truth of what actually matters.

Ultimately, we are not looking for guidance about making the everyday decisions about whether to do A or B. We can put up with the occasional setbacks and we accept that we will suffer from pain, depression and grief from time to time. We presume that we will sometimes, hopefully, be happy, possibly even ecstatic but none of this is ultimately important - it is simply part of day to day life. What we are really looking for is some context to give our lives meaning beyond the transient ups and downs. We would like to have some overall understanding that could reassure us that this is not all that there is; that life itself, if not our own life *per se*, has some significance. Ideally we would like to know that our existence is more than accidental and will continue beyond the death of this body. These are what really matters and this book aims to give you answers that you will find both intellectually satisfying and existentially meaningful.

When we ask ourselves the question "what should I do?" there is probably the desire to turn towards someone who, we believe, will be able to give us a satisfying answer. The writer and philosopher Jean-Paul Sartre claimed that the person to whom we eventually turn is usually chosen because we anticipate that he or she is likely to give us the answer that we want, consciously or otherwise. We seek to free ourselves from the responsibility of deciding for ourselves. A psychologist will rationalize everything in terms of your childhood or sublimated desires or whatever; a member of the local church is almost certainly going to start talking about God, sin and the afterlife. Parents will be interested in your "making something of your life" rather than simply enjoying it; dependent relatives may have their own mercenary motives at the back of their mind. Ultimately, we would like to be in possession of all of the relevant information so that we may make up our own minds. This book aims to satisfy that need.

I hope to demonstrate to you that, in all of the questions that you ask about life and your place in it, you are effectively missing the point. You assign inappropriate values to things and events, believing that they will bring you happiness when, in, fact they can never do so. By all means continue to ask yourself such questions as "What is really important to me?" and "What do I want out of my life?" but do not attempt to answer them until you have finished reading the book!

2. Meaning – filling the holes in our lives

When we talk about wasting time, perhaps what really concerns us at the back of our minds is that we are effectively wasting our lives. Most of us firmly believe that we are this body-mind-person and that we have but a short life between its birth and death. We want to make the most of the relatively brief time that is available to us, to feel that we are spending it meaningfully and not frittering it away.

If we just flop down on the sofa and spend a couple of hours watching a video, whose only merit is its escapist entertainment, we are likely to feel a bit uneasy about it on subsequent reflection. We may well justify it to ourselves along the lines of "well, I've been working hard all day – I need to unwind." Though we may not admit it to everyone, however, we probably feel that this type of activity is somehow simply time-filling. It does not provide us with any justification in terms of "meaning."

If, on the other hand, we had spent the time painting a picture or in some other, "creative" pursuit, we would quite likely feel that it had been time well spent and have no subsequent pangs of guilt. We even have phrases for it, such as spending "quality time" with our children. What exactly do we mean and how do we find this "meaning"?

The Pathetique mood

When I was much younger, and especially whilst at university, I used frequently to fall to wondering about life and its apparent pointlessness. I knew at the time that the main reason for this was that I saw the few friends I had spending all their spare time socializing, going out drinking and partying, having lots of other friends and generally giving the appearance of enjoying themselves. The most relevant factor of all was related to friends of the opposite sex or, in my own case, the absence of these. I was attracted to several and agonized over my inability to meet them in natural surroundings, engage them in meaningful conversation and get to know them.

Finding myself alone in my lodgings, I would sink into a depression, philosophize in a narrow, egotistical sense and even try to write poetry. I called these my Pathetique moods, because I would choose to listen to music such as Tchaikovsky's 6th Symphony. The sentiments seemed to match my own. On the third movement, I had this to say: *'the passive acceptance interspersed with aggressive but ultimately futile striving; a yearning for the unobtainable; beautiful sadness, reveling in misery"*. When this movement ended, I noted *"Oh God, 4th movement! Perhaps shouldn't listen to this"* and at the conclusion: *'terrible ending, complete resignation – bullet through brain?"'*.

It seemed to me then that everyone was, in a sense, living a lie. My friends never seemed to think about anything serious. Socially, they only spoke about inconsequential matters. I recognized that there was a certain degree of bias here, i.e. what I really meant was that their topics of conversation usually did not interest me. I was prepared to admit that, had they been of interest, I might well have taken part and even deluded myself that I was enjoying them. And it was this consideration that led me to what seemed an inescapable conclusion, namely that people sought out distractions of this sort in order to avoid the feelings that I was having.

Later, I attempted to express such ideas more clearly. I reasoned that man's basic state is one of depression, facing up to the fact that there is no meaning to our lives. In order to avoid this awful admission, it is inevitable that we turn towards involvement. We aim to keep our minds constantly active. *"Providing the mind is ... directed in a particular sphere ... we have no time to ponder upon the pointlessness of being here. Mixing with people, enjoying oneself, doing things (of no consequence) distracts the mind from the underlying futility. Life draws a blind over reality."* If we don't continually divert ourselves in this way, we find ourselves in wretched despair.

In fact, in this experience, I missed the opportunity for gaining a much deeper insight. I actually missed the main point completely. I was condemning all of those other people for their trivial pursuits and feeling sorry for them that they had allowed themselves to be deluded into thinking their activities to be worthwhile. At the same time I was secretly envying their relative happiness (and studies have consistently shown that extraverts are happier than introverts). And herein was my mistake - I believed that their happiness was self-delusion and that my misery was real.

It was probably true that I was thinking more deeply about what actually matters in life and how one ought to lead it, and I do not regret having wasted time then because the misery was the prompt to investigate all of these questions in later life. Whilst we are happy, there is simply no incentive to ask why and risk undermining that happiness. But it was not until more than thirty years later that I finally understood the key to the whole problem. It is partly explained by the fact that depression is usually associated with a low self-esteem and, although we use the word "low" here, what this really means is a high awareness of ego – constantly thinking about me. In such a situation, it is not unusual to react by thinking that everyone else is in the wrong. The key is the ego, but you will have to wait until much later in the book to find out how this fact can unlock anything.

Keeping busy

I am certain that many people effectively pursue a "keep busy" philosophy, if it could be called that, without necessarily realizing it. After all, if your life is so active – from waking in the morning and plunging into the going-to-work routine, to falling into bed after going out drinking or to a club or whatever more sophisticated amusement you may indulge in – there is simply no *time* to start thinking about whether it is all worth the effort. Another way of looking at this is that most people are so busy "doing" that they simply have no time to think about meaning. But which is cause and which effect might be debated. Younger people may say that they will start worrying about this sort of thing later in life when they have the time (or can no longer find the stamina!).

You would be hard put to find a more attractive, vivacious, intelligent and caring young lady than my stepdaughter. She has an interesting and worthwhile job and has active ecological and humanitarian interests. She has many friends and is always arranging activities or participating in events organized by others. She recently took a year out to find out what life was like in other parts of the world. And I could go on – but that is the point. She is always doing something and, more particularly, feels uncomfortable in the rare event that she does not specifically have something to do next. And it seems, though I have not discussed this with her, that a recent event confirms this view. A few years ago, she began with apparent enthusiasm to read the draft of my last book (which is a much more academic treatment of the philosophy underlying the ideas that will be expressed in this book). But, after fewer than ten pages, by which time the subject matter had become apparent, after raising a good point about one particular aspect, she seemed to lose interest and did not read any more.

For many their overall peace of mind, assuming they have such a thing to begin with, is maintained by not disturbing the status quo. If you have a full life, it is likely that you will be generally happy. Naturally, events will occur that disturb this from time to time: an illness, a bill to be paid, a falling-out with a friend etc. But these are essentially ripples on the pond and, after all, are effectively yet more things to occupy your mind and keep you from thinking about things too deeply. You may not have the answers but, if you never get around to asking the questions, perhaps it doesn't matter too much!

People worry about all sorts of things. In our day to day life there will always be something whose importance raises it above the background noise. These are the personal problems that everyone has to put up with at one time or another, whether it be toothache or worry about a forthcoming stressful event at work. Then there are always current topics of more general interest that are potential causes for concern. Listen to the news on the radio for the ones of the moment. As I write this, for example, the police are still looking for leads in relation to the disappearance of two small girls and there are views being voiced about the forthcoming conference on pollution. Should we actively worry about the Asian Brown Haze, the layer of pollution from vehicles, factories and controlled burning of forests that is poisoning the atmosphere in Singapore and elsewhere?

Some people, who either do not have problems of their own to worry about or whose nature makes them take an interest in more global concerns, frequently divert energy into finding out about such matters and campaigning in whatever way they feel able. Is this something all of us *ought* to be doing? Certainly the campaigners would say so. In this particular example, they would argue that it is *our* world and that we owe it to future generations to ensure that it is environmentally safe for them. If everyone takes the attitude that it is someone else's responsibility, then this will not happen. And so on!

And I am not disagreeing with or condemning such an attitude. But then I do not intend to write much about such things either. In the context of what I am saying at present, all of such endeavors are diversions. They are issues over which we can argue at length and on which we can expend (i.e. waste) considerable efforts. They may indeed occupy us for an entire lifetime, fill us with a sense of purpose and provide a degree of happiness. But is this sufficient? I would maintain that they take us away from the ultimate question of our *raison d'être*. It does seem to be that it is only when you are in a prolonged situation where life is not filled in ways such as these that you begin to wonder whether your own existence is ultimately of value.

Most of our actions and endeavors have some purpose in mind. When we get up on a typical working day, our immediate purpose will be to shower, have breakfast etc., then to get in the car and drive to work and so on. Trivial activities tend to have short-term goals but these combine into overall objectives. We go to work in order to earn money, preferably whilst doing something that is not too tedious. Some fortunate people actually derive satisfaction from their jobs so that going to work is itself fulfilling. Many more simply go to work because they have to, in order to obtain the other things that provide meaning, a certain acceptable standard of living and an annual holiday.

Perhaps some find meaning in life from a particular hobby and can hardly wait to retire so that they can spend the remainder of their lives in that pursuit. Is this really a *meaning*? Are we justified in saying it is not? What about someone who spends all of their free time working in an al-Qaeda cell? They will have short-term meaning and long term purpose, no doubt. If it is meaningful for them, can we condemn it (from their point of view)? We might prefer it if they confined their unsociable activities to getting drunk and shouting at the opposing football teams - but then that would be less meaningful to them, wouldn't it?

There is also the question of our long-term aspirations, whose attainment would (we think) make our lives seem to be worthwhile in our own minds. Thus, someone may apparently lead a very full life, always doing something, with every action having a purpose leading towards some planned event in the near future and still that person may feel that his or her life is entirely without any overall meaning. Conversely, someone else may appear to do very little, have a mundane job and no social life and yet, perhaps because of their spiritual beliefs, feel that their life is full of meaning. One presumes that monks and others, who live their lives entirely within a closed religious community and do little more than tend the garden and pray, are nevertheless likely to feel fulfilled, devoting themselves to their God.

The meaning of meaning

We ought to be sure that we understand the words we are using before we continue much further. Suppose that someone said you were noetic or called you Argus-eyed. Unless you were taught Greek at school or read extensively, you might well take offence or even wonder if you ought to visit the doctor. (In fact, the former would imply that you tend to indulge in intellectual speculation while the latter says that you are watchful and vigilant, after the hundred-eyed watchman of Greek mythology.) The point is obvious. If communication is to take place effectively, it is necessary that both speaker and listener have the same under-standing of the terms being used.

Languages have been around for a long time now. Some people are fortunate to receive a good education. They learn something about the etymology of the words that we use so that a good appreciation of their original meaning is gained. Most, however, merely intuit the sense of words from their context, often misunderstanding them and then passing this confusion on to others so that time twists the definition into something new. And, over time, the ways in which people use particular words can change dramatically. We will see, for example, how a word such as "person" has come to mean the exact opposite of what was originally intended.

This is not always a problem, of course. Newly invented words can mean whatever we define them to mean (though it is always best to pay due attention to the meanings of the various sounds in the word). This happens all the time in the area of science, with each new discovery or advance in technology. We can create entirely novel combinations of letters or re-use existing words in different ways. As long as we all agree what we are doing to begin with, it does not matter too much. But where a meaning changes as it has with the word "person", so that the original and new meaning are at odds, misunderstanding can arise. Similar problems occur when I use a word in one sense when I speak to you and you understand it in a quite different sense.

I recall reading once of the following unfortunate (if somewhat implausible) situation. A family from the North of England was on holiday in the South. They were driving along a country lane when they encountered a railroad crossing. Instead of a gate, it had lights at each side of the railway line, with a sign saying "**Do not cross while lights are flashing**." Being very law-abiding, they switched off the engine and sat there patiently for a very long time until, when the lights began to flash, they restarted the vehicle and continued on their way. The point was that, in Lancashire and Yorkshire, certainly amongst older generations, the word "while" is used in the sense of "until." Grandma might tell the child, for example, if she wants to play outside but it happens to be raining, "Y'll 'ave to stay in lass, while t'sun comes out!"

Things may, however, be much worse than this. Many have argued, especially in the last century, that language is fundamental to problems of philosophy. Clearly this must be so in the sense discussed above. If we are arguing about some thorny problem, we are not going to get very far unless we both have the same understanding of the terms we are using. But isn't the same thing going to happen in our own thinking? Our thoughts are themselves language-based. If we have fundamentally misunderstood some term, which we are endeavoring to use in our own mental arguments, we are not going to reach any satisfactory conclusion. It would be like trying to solve a mathematical equation. If we used the wrong definition, we couldn't expect to get the right answer. The philosopher Wittgenstein claimed that many of the so-called problems in life would vanish if they were simply stated correctly. Attempts to talk about God, emotional problems and so on, he said, where there are no concrete facts to which the language can relate are ultimately meaningless. He ended the only work that was published in his lifetime (which goes by the wonderful name of "Tractatus Logico-Philosophicus") with the oft-quoted statement: *"Whereof we cannot speak, thereof we should remain silent"*.

The meaning of life

Bearing all of this in mind, we ought first of all to ask what we mean by "meaning" in a question such as "What is the meaning of life?" before asking the question itself. It might make sense to ask "what is the meaning of this abstract painting?", since it is the creation of an artist who perhaps had some specific idea or purpose in mind before and during the execution. But does it make equal sense to ask: "what is the meaning of this earthquake?" The sciences of seismology and geology may be able to say quite a lot about what happened and why but do these explanations constitute meaning? If our understanding of this word includes some concept of purpose then the only context in which it could make sense would be if we believed in a divine being who was the cause behind all natural events (and presumably unnatural ones, too).

It might make sense to ask "What is the meaning of *my* life?" in the sense of looking for some personal ambition or objective. What do *I* want out of this existence? We usually take it for granted that I have freedom of will and can choose to act in one way rather than another. Although I might have been a software-engineer all of my working life, I believe I can decide to drop all of this and become a full-time writer. But does it make any sense to ask: "what is the meaning of the life of the tree in my garden"? Purpose, will and freedom seem to go together and most of us would probably argue that only human beings have all of these. Isn't life itself a mindless process, without intelligence in the sense that we normally use the word? You might also want to ask why you should want to live a life that is meaningful, though if you seriously did wonder about this, it is most unlikely that you would be reading this book, so I won't pursue that one!

A thesaurus gives the following basic categories for the word "meaning": *definition; drift; effect; force; impact; implication; import; message; matter; point; rhyme; sense; significance; spirit; substance; tenor.* All of these ways of understanding the word itself ultimately relate to us. If we are honest, we have to admit that what we want to know when we ask the question is how we are to live our own life. There are two elements to this. One is to determine a style of living that brings satisfaction and a feeling that continued living is worthwhile irrespective of whether there is any ultimate purpose. This is perhaps a good definition of the word "meaning" in the context used in this book – an ongoing rationale for one's day to day life. The second is to establish a final aim, to be achieved before one dies, possibly at the expense of any satisfaction here and now. This definition relates more to the idea of purpose as discussed later – an overall objective, which acts as a beacon but from which we may diverge from time to time. In a sense, ultimate goals continue beyond the grave. We want perhaps to create a work of art that, by its envisaged admiration by future generations, will provide us now with a sense of immortality.

Lou Marinoff gives an excellent metaphor in his book on philosophical counseling, *Plato not Prozac*. This relates to someone going into a foreign restaurant to order some food. If he does not understand the language, the menu will have no meaning even though its purpose is understood. If he is able to read it but the prices are so high that he cannot afford to buy anything, then it will have meaning but no purpose. Someone who has never heard of restaurants or menus will find neither meaning nor purpose. It is also possible to confuse meaning and purpose by eating the menu!

Is this all there is?

When it comes to life, meaning and purpose are inextricably linked. If we believe that "this is all that there is", then we are reduced to thinking in terms of maximizing pleasure and minimizing pain; of making our life in the society in which we move as comfortable as possible. Albert Camus, the Nobel prize-winning novelist, believed that there is no meaning at all in the universe and said that any attempt to make sense of our lives is consequently absurd. In one of his philosophical essays, he compares our situation to that of the character Sisyphus from Greek mythology, whose sentence in hell was repeatedly to push a boulder up to the top of a mountain, from which it always rolled down again.

The options for any kind of meaning beyond my death seem to be limited to some sort of achievement now, that will result in others' recognizing my name in the future, or in passing on my genes to children who may succeed in this manner. Both of these options could provide a boost to my ego but is this what we mean by a sense of purpose? Again, it seems somewhat hollow and ultimately unsatisfactory. The evolutionary psychologist will argue that the genetic aspect is in fact the real answer. Those ways of behaving in the past are the ones that have proven to be successful – they must have been otherwise the related genes would not have been passed on. Ergo, this is what will continue to happen until a random mutation produces a gene that confers additional advantage.

Your attitude will be completely different if you disagree with Camus and believe in some sort of life after death, a reward in the future for the way that you behave now. People who have suffered adversities such as the death of a close family member, divorce, serious illness etc. are seen to cope better and recover more quickly if they are believers. Their outlook on life in general is positive and more of them will tend to describe themselves as happy than similarly affected non-believers. One series of interviews concluded that those who regarded their religion as the most important influence in their lives were twice as likely to claim to be very happy as those who were not particularly religious.

And it seems not to matter whether people are rationally able to defend their beliefs. As long as they are practicing, attending church regularly, and following the relevant rituals, the security of the metaphysical basis for those beliefs seems not to be so important. If we act as though it were all true, this seems to have the desired effect. It is probably the case for the majority of those attached to any religion that they never seriously question the tenets. The essential practices have been inculcated into them from early childhood and are simply accepted. This naïve submission suffices to provide the background of meaning and anticipation of ultimate fulfillment to carry them through all but the most severe of life's tribulations.

Pop-psychology

People who are not religious also lack the external source of justification and support. It is hardly surprising then that many turn to pseudo-scientific authorities that promise ways of instilling meaning and purpose into their lives. Since there is no God to help you, they claim implicitly, you must help yourselves "with the help of this scientifically proven technique, which I will share with you for the give-away price of only $10."

These fad techniques, loudly hyped in the ad pages of popular magazines and newspapers and highly visible in the self-help sections of bookshops, are touted as methods for cultivating positive thinking. They purport to change our attitudes and personalities, turning us from people who submissively accept life's adversities into dynamic individuals who make life go our own way. In the past ten or twenty years, even businesses have been taken in by such approaches, rightly acknowledging that an energetic and motivated workforce would be highly beneficial for profits.

But it always seems that, when such systems are exposed to scientific examination under controlled conditions, the claims are shown to be unfounded. It usually turns out to be like the placebo effect with drugs or the Hawthorne Effect. (This relates to the productivity experiments carried out between 1927 and 1932 in the US. The social scientist Elton Mayo wanted to test the effect of the ambient lighting on the productivity of textile workers. It was found that productivity increased for both the test group and the control group and later tests discovered that it continued to increase no matter what changes they made to the environmental factors. It was eventually realized that the workers were gaining motivation merely because someone was taking an interest in them.)

Thus someone who believes, for whatever misguided reasons, that something will help achieve a particular goal is likely to find that it *does* help. When subjected to controlled experiments, however, it is usually found that the subject only *believes* that he is performing better, In actual fact, there is no change. It is simply a matter of boosting the ego and bringing about self-delusion – for a while. Once the novelty wears off, the situation is back to where it was before. Except that in the long run, one is likely to believe that if several approaches have failed then one is *oneself* a failure.

But if one of the effects is that we feel happier, then you might say it is not entirely a placebo, even if the actual claims are not being met. For a full explanation of what is happening in such cases, you will have to wait until the discussion on happiness. Briefly though, if self-help books of this type help us to delude ourselves into thinking we have indeed achieved the desired outcome, then the related desire goes away – and this is one of the keys to being happy.

So, in the end paradoxically, pop psychology is not totally worthless. Thinking positively *does* prove beneficial. It takes us out of ourselves, stops us from being self-conscious or self-centered. Those who have a perpetually pessimistic outlook on life are clearly not happy. If reading positively written words helps us to cultivate a more optimistic frame of mind, then it may at least promote happiness indirectly.

Another phrase that often crops up in the mind-body-spirit shelves in modern bookstores is "finding oneself." In effect, this is the principal subject of this book but the meaning here is a literal one – discovering who we truly are, as opposed to what we normally think ourselves to be. In the case of the vast majority of pop-psychology usage, what is actually meant is the discovering of satisfaction in one's life. This, in turn, may be reworded to say that such books are aiming to provide boosts to self-confidence, ways of realizing ambitions, finding the perfect partner and so on. I.e. the majority of books that use this phrase are talking about ways of reinforcing the ego, making it less susceptible to criticism, more resilient and subtle in the ways in which it influences us and the world around us. Following such a road is a very grave mistake indeed and the precise opposite to the intent of this book.

The root problem here, as far as modern western society is concerned, is the increased importance being placed upon the individual. We are all encouraged to pursue our own interests and endeavors in order to find fulfillment. All of the earlier values of family or workplace or community have been supplanted by values relating to self. We are now the selfish society and it is perfectly acceptable to much of the present generation that we can justify our behavior and aims in life simply on the grounds that it is something that *I* want to do. If I don't like my job, home or partner, I will go elsewhere. We are each unique, we are told, and have a right to discover and express our individuality. Individualism is, of course, simply the modern euphemism for egoism. It is ironic that, on the basis of such beliefs, we are encouraged by pop-psychology to discover ourselves, realize our potential and so on when it is precisely these false conceptions that will prevent us from ever doing so.

With myself as clearly the most important aspect of life regardless of how this may impact upon others, it is hardly surprising that today's society is finding itself in trouble in so many areas, from rising crime and drug-abuse through to increasing divorce rates and suicides. The incidence of depression alone has increased tenfold in just two generations. Respect for parents, elders, lawmakers and enforcers, etc. have all inevitably fallen as this sense of self-importance has increased. The idea that "I know best" is drilled into us from all sides and from the earliest age.

Death – when time runs out

It seems to us that our opportunities to discover meaning diminish as we grow older, our bodies less able to indulge in physical enjoyments and our minds becoming increasingly feeble, even if we succeed in avoiding senility. Death itself is the finishing post. If we haven't identified, pursued, and achieved our unique purpose in life before then, we have failed. This seems to be the inevitable conclusion.

In a sense it could be argued (and many have) that, in the end, it is concern over our own inevitable death that is at the root of our worries. Schopenhauer, though admittedly one of our more depressing philosophers, said: "*Undoubtedly, it is the knowledge of death, and therewith the consideration of the suffering and misery of life, that give the strongest impulse to philosophical reflection and metaphysical explanations of the world.*" There is no doubt that, of all of the things we have to worry about that affect us most immediately, our death has few to beat it. If we have to worry about something, that is as good a topic as any. And perhaps there is some truth in any theory that argues that many other concerns, such as recognition by others, are stimulated by worries over our continued existence. After all, if everyone ignores us, perhaps we might as well be dead.

At present, you may relate your sense of purpose to the extent to which you are able to influence or be acknowledged by this external world. Almost certainly any failure or lack you feel will be a result of the degree to which you feel this has not been achieved. Most of us depend upon this world and other people for our justification. We believe, without any foundation whatsoever, that the world must have a meaning. Although we may not claim that it has been created by a God in order to provide us with an environment in which to develop our soul, we probably nevertheless feel that there must be some purpose not yet discovered by science.

The existential viewpoint on death might be represented as follows:

Before our birth we were nothing and after our death we will be nothing. Death brings an end to all possibilities and, in a sense, makes everything meaningless. We have to face this fact, accept responsibility for our life here and now, and then act without procrastination. Our lives are in a sense defined by the nothingness that forever threatens in the background.

But meaning is something that *we* impose upon the changing world in order to make it more acceptable. It is not something intrinsic in the universe itself. Ultimately, it is only a concept through which we see and interpret what is happening. If the concept is stable, we can delude ourselves into thinking that the external situation too is stable and therefore under our control. And, to some degree, this ploy can be effective. An example is the use of the concept of marriage, which we use to impose guidance and stability upon the changing relationship between two people. Even life is such a concept, from the "mewling and puking infant" to the "second childishness" of old age. As will be seen later, exactly where *we* come into this progression is rather difficult to ascertain.

Traditional sources of meaning

You don't really need anyone to tell you that much of your thinking is influenced by your upbringing. Initially, your parents are the source of most of your attitudes and beliefs. When they tell you that *this* is the way things are, you are in no position to contradict them. Soon, teachers, television and friends will begin to add their views to the forces molding your ideas and feelings. Sometimes, you might even wonder whether you have any opinions that are truly your own!

Most societies before today's technological, materialistic and individualistic one were largely religious. When the distribution of wealth meant that most people were unable to satisfy desires that required significant amounts of money, it was perhaps inevitable that meanings had to be found elsewhere. If fulfillment was not to be found in this life, then it was clearly useful to be able to believe in an afterlife that would reward those who behaved appropriately.

We almost certainly delude ourselves when we think that people used to be happy in the good old days. In fact the days were never particularly good – many of them were *very* much worse – and people were no happier then, on average, than they are now. Choices were usually severely restricted in the past. People tended to accept the existing traditions, following their parents' ways of life and work. If one was born into a particular stratum of society, it was extremely difficult to move outside of this, as readers of books such as Thomas Hardy's *Jude the Obscure* will know. Accepting this and committing oneself to a life of being a stonemason, for example, could bring fulfillment and happiness. One could find satisfaction through performing the work faultlessly and artistically and fulfillment through looking back at one's work in later life. Rejecting all of this and attempting to become a scholar would almost certainly bring misery.

People were similarly restricted in their choice of company. They would generally marry someone from their own village and most likely stay with them for the rest of their life, regardless of compatibility. This would seem unacceptably limiting to us now, and a potential cause for great unhappiness, but the fact that this was taken for granted meant that people did not rebel against it and adapted their outlook accordingly. Even today, it is often found that the arranged marriages of Muslims, for example, are statistically happier than ones where partners are freely chosen.

But most of us now believe that choices have to be freely made, not imposed by family or made because the prevailing mood of one's peers or society is that it is the preferred one. We feel that choices must be made by each person as necessary. In the context of one's life, there can be no single purpose suitable for all at all times. Unique circumstances, desires and limitations always have to be taken into account.

The area most often associated with achievement today is a person's career. (It is amusing to note the meaning of the verb "career" – to move swiftly and *in an uncontrolled way* in a specified direction.) Some merely regard it as going to work, of course, as a way of earning money, and not as something that brings gratification and happiness in its own right. In the days prior to the industrial revolution an artisan, having learned a particular trade, could derive satisfaction from providing a service to others through a specialized skill in which he might excel and thereby find fulfillment. Relating directly with others utilizing one's service, there would be immediate feedback and appreciation, providing a clear sense of self-worth. Similarly, farmers would be working much more directly with the land, without the aid of mechanization and chemicals, harvesting their food to sell directly to neighbors in the markets, not to faceless multi-nationals. The increasing depersonalization and industrialization has led to many jobs becoming merely a means to an end and not seeming to have any intrinsic value.

With the appearance of factories and the spread of transport systems for selling goods outside of the immediate locality, many jobs lost their potential for providing any sense of achievement. Repetitious, assembly line work is arduous, boring and distinctly unfulfilling. The conditions for such employment have improved significantly but people who have such jobs are usually forced to look to hobbies and other outside activities as sources of genuine satisfaction.

There may be a higher level of material comfort in the modern world than there has ever been before but this is not matched by the degree of spiritual fulfillment. Traditional religions no longer seem to satisfy the numbers that they once did. In the past the priests and rabbis would provide all of the answers to our spiritual needs, providing that the questions were not too searching. The values of religion once impacted on practically all aspects of one's lives. People were in general told what to believe and, whether or not they were interested in such matters, generally followed that guidance.

People have naturally always been interested in discovering meaning in their lives. Suffering used to be an accepted fact for most, with few material comforts to lessen the harshness of life in general and little in the way of medicine to prevent illness and early death. Believing in some divine purpose (even if this purpose is not itself known), which puts all of this into context, lessens the significance of our personal hardships and consequently helps alleviate such suffering. History shows that people are more than ready to delude themselves in order to satisfy this need, whether through organized religions, cults or simply by being superstitious.

Accordingly, it seems that we have an in-built predisposition towards believing in a religion, irrespective of how much truth it might actually contain. With the foundational security of a context and explanation for our lives, we can then get on with the business of living them. We need to feel that the world is, to some degree, comprehensible and not fundamentally threatening. Ideally, we would always be in control of our environment but the next best thing is to understand what is happening. Then we can at least have the illusion of being in charge of our destiny.

To many people, searching for, or feeling that one has, a purpose in life, *means* to be religious. The meaning of the word is "to bind" (*ligare*) "again" or "back" (*re*). What we are connecting to is our real nature or the truth, something that we already know but have forgotten. It does seem reasonable to suppose that we need this basis of truth and reality out of which we might construct meaning within our own lives. So although the ideas that we have about religion may no longer seem relevant today, the true meaning of the word will always be relevant and is what we will always be looking for – even if we do not realize this!

The meaning is "within" not in a literal sense of course but with the purport of discovering our real nature, finding out who we truly are. Any search for meaning in external objects, events or other people is doomed to failure – the truth is never going to be found "out there."

The material society

The advent of science marked the boundary between the old world and the modern. It did not however open the way towards any understanding of self or purpose or make us more satisfied with what we had. In fact, it led towards materialism and an ever-increasing concentration on detail. Instead of looking inwards, the world of objectivity was suddenly opened up in ways that had previously been unimaginable. It was now possible to continue to find out more and more about less and less, as someone once cynically pointed out, until in the end we will know everything about nothing. Discoveries and inventions have diverted us ever since, making life easier and perhaps more enjoyable but doing little to explain to us what exactly it is really about. Where would we be without the automobile, refrigerator, television and the atomic bomb? How would we survive if we couldn't look forward to holidays in the Bahamas and choosing the sex of our future children?

In the past 40 years, the number and quality of material possessions and the general standard of living may have increased dramatically, with most people now owning all of the modern necessities such as cars, videos and mobile phones. We have money to go out to clubs, cinemas and restaurants. But amidst all of the affluence, divorce and suicide rates soar. Doctors hand out more and more Prozac and fight losing battles against drug and alcohol addiction. It seems that increasing numbers of people are failing to find any meaning in their lives. And, instead of questioning the whole ethos of the materialistic culture, many people still feel that the way out of their dissatisfaction is to get even more money so that they can stay ahead of their contemporaries, escape to a different location or country, or simply not have to worry about where their next luxury is coming from.

Over 150 years ago, Karl Marx recognized that so-called progress had produced a world of technology but man was being controlled by this instead of controlling it. Mankind was being alienated from the true values of life, such as friendship and culture, and instead was being conned into desiring the products themselves. In this process, it was inevitable that man should feel that he himself was becoming dehumanized. Most of us probably now appreciate that cars, CDs and mobile phones, are mere things that can never bring happiness or fulfillment. And yet many in today's generation seem to be trapped in a downward spiral of dependence upon the next fix from the purveyors of our material society.

Others, however, are realizing that this never-ending escalation of ambition and achievement is not the answer. Manically working long hours six or seven days a week may bring short term rewards and certainly more money but it leads to tiredness, ulcers and broken relationships – apart from the fact that you have no time to actually enjoy the extra money. What is the point in developing drugs to cure diseases and increase longevity if we are not happy for the duration of the lives that we currently have? If we are less happy now than our ancestors, perhaps we should be more concerned with nature than with civilization, with pursuing spiritual rather than material values.

Most people make plans for their future, whether this takes the form of deciding where to go on holiday next year or choosing to which school to send their child. To this extent life clearly has a meaning for them. But, whereas the religious person might believe that there is an ultimate purpose imposed by a God upon their existence, most people try to establish their own meaning. They decide which things are important, which of the myriad potential goals are attainable, desirable and worthwhile, and plan their lives to work towards them. Unfortunately, these decisions are usually influenced by society, which today means that most people are aiming at material goals. If we get them, we may feel good... but only for a short time.

Living for the moment

Many seem to be satisfied with having only meaning in their lives. They can happily admit that there is no purpose. Our being here is entirely accidental. When we die, that is an end to it. Whether we spend our lives in continual search for personal pleasure or whether we sacrifice all of this and spend our time trying to help others makes no difference ultimately to anyone. Live for the moment and get as much out of it as you can – this often seems to be the slogan of today's materialistic society. And it is not only a modern phenomenon. After the horrors and privations of the First World War, the natural reaction was the hedonism of the Roaring Twenties with many people living life to the utmost in the moment, heedless of a now uncertain future. It certainly seems that we need to have some stability and normality in our daily lives (meaning) before we can reasonably start to think about an overall purpose.

After all, if we had a map of the area where we happened to be, we would have to be able to read and understand the map before we could work out where we wanted to go.

Living for the moment, in its usually accepted sense of pleasure seeking, is fine as long as the moment lasts for ever. Of course it never does and, once the gap between the emotional highs starts to lengthen, the hedonistic creed is likely to be seen in its true shallowness. It is then that more searching questions are asked. What is the significance of our being here? What impact have we had on our fellow beings? Will there be any effect when we have gone? Should I be exerting all of my efforts towards a specific goal and, if so, what is it? Are there any considerations beyond the merely human? Is there, dare we ask it, a God? If so, what purpose does *He* have in mind or does it not make any sense to ask such things?

Questions such as these lead on to other, equally difficult ones. Assuming that some courses of action are in some way *better* than others (according to what criteria?), can we actually choose to follow those? Are we *free* to act however we like? Even more fundamental than this, can we actually *do* anything at all? People, who have not given any real thought to questions such as these, may be tempted to respond with incredulity. They *know* that they can continue to read this book or not. Is it not obvious that we have free will in this sense? When you throw the book down in disgust and get up to make a cup of coffee, *you* are doing these things, are you not? Certainly no one else is doing them. Is it not obvious then that we act? These are topics that must be addressed and resolved if we are to get anywhere with our basic questions and we will look at them in detail in later chapters.

3. Purpose – making our lives seem complete

We may delude ourselves for a long time into thinking that our life is satisfactory, if we are constantly able to fill up our time with activity. Even if what we are doing is not something that we might freely choose to do, if it requires our attention then our mind is not free to dwell on those things that it might prefer that we were doing. And if the activity *is* enjoyable, then it is likely that we will simply relish the pleasure while it lasts and it would be strange indeed if we were to wish to be doing something else. But there are inevitably moments when we are not busy, when the mind suddenly looks around, as it were, and says to itself: "What am I doing here? Ought I to be doing something else entirely? Is what I am doing ultimately worthwhile?"

Day to day meaning in our lives is all very well, and many would be very pleased to be able to claim that they had this. But, in the end, it is never enough. We want a sense of purpose. In the imagination of the popular cliché, we want to be able to look back at the end of our life and feel that it has been worthwhile; perhaps have achieved something that will be recognized and appreciated by future generations. We do not want to think that life itself is meaningless or that our own might just as well never have happened.

What do *I* want?

First of all, let us agree that this seems to be fundamental to the issue of what matters in life as far as I am concerned. It is what *I* want, not what anyone else wants or what is best for the world. Some people may claim that everything that they do is for someone else - a son, daughter or other relative for example. But in most cases, this will be because the welfare of the other is what gives them the most satisfaction or feeling of worth in life or because they feel responsibility or guilt. Unselfishness is usually selfishness in disguise. There *are* people of the caliber of Mother Theresa in the world but we do not meet them very often.

There must be times when you just don't feel like doing anything. Not because you are tired or ill but for no immediately obvious reason at all. Or maybe you do know why – a recent disappointment, divorce, death of a relation or any number of other causes has plunged you into a depression. Intellectually you know it is unreasonable or at least that there is nothing you can do about the situation. Practically speaking, you simply have to get on with life until it passes. Emotions rule however, and no amount of cajoling, whether from yourself or from others, can snap you out of it. In such a situation, *nothing* matters. You simply wallow aimlessly in a mire of indecision, where all perceptions are washed out and all feelings numbed.

Fortunately, for most of us such times are few. They pass and we are soon turning outwards again, taking an interest in others and in the events around us. And this can often go to the other extreme. We become passionately interested in some event, objective, person etc. to the point of obsession. Though there are many other things we know we ought to be doing, we cannot stop ourselves from spending all of our waking moments thinking about, planning for, working towards the thing that we feel *really* matters.

Clearly these situations relate to purely subjective concerns and we would not want to claim that they were important in any absolute sense. We may often delude ourselves that the things that concern us are genuinely important. It is usually the case, though, that everything that we believe matters does so only in respect of the degree to which it affects, or might affect, us personally. Those aspects deemed to be most important tend to be close to home, directly relating to ourselves, our work or our family and friends. As we move outwards to town and country, the importance tends to diminish unless there is still the potential to affect us eventually. Thus we might object to a proposal to build a landfill site anywhere within, say, a ten mile radius. If it were a nuclear waste dump, we might not be happy with a hundred miles.

Issues such as global warming ought perhaps to interest us all, making us anxious for future generations even though we may not be immediately affected. But so often this tends to be hypothetical. One scientist says that England will be partially flooded as the sea rises as a result of melting ice. Another claims that the Gulf Stream will be disrupted, causing the English Channel to freeze over in winter. The fact is that what matters does so because we know that it affects us (or those who matter to us) directly or because it is believed that it will affect us (or them) in the foreseeable future. We may grunt over our Cornflakes when we read of some remote Pacific island being flattened by a hurricane but it is usually forgotten the next minute.

Things can only really matter *to us*. If they do not and cannot affect us, and providing that we do not imagine that they might in the future, then they do not matter at all. There is no such thing as an objective "mattering." Just as the Pacific islanders do not worry about the additional runways being built at Heathrow, so we do not worry that their village has just been flattened. When the Vogons arrive to blow up the earth to make way for a new hyperspace bypass, it simply will not matter in the slightest to the residents of Splxalytl in the Andromeda galaxy. They might click their antennae disapprovingly as they hear about it on the hyper-waves over their dish of minced sand-worms but they will have forgotten all about it by the next minute.

What do I have to do to be happy?

Most people think that they know what they want out of life. Often we imagine that unlimited supplies of money would solve everything. Maybe we think we would like prestige or power (or perhaps we feel that such things will come along with the money anyway). But do any of these things actually entail happiness? We might well be prepared to give them a try, given the opportunity, but perhaps we should consider whether it is not simply the case that we have been conned by society into thinking that they are a necessary precursor of happiness. Maybe it is not the case at all and they have simply become symbols of happiness to the materialistically minded West. It would be naïve to suppose that having money does not ease the burden of life. After all, if you don't have money, you may well be obliged to worry about all of the basics such as accommodation and food. But we also know that (as the purveyors of folk wisdom repeatedly tell us) "money is not everything." Happiness and perceived meaning are much more important.

Most Westerners today probably do not believe that there is any ultimate purpose to life in general. They deny that there is a God whose will should be obeyed or that there is an afterlife in which actions in this life will be rewarded or punished. But most will feel that they know what they themselves want in order to feel they have led a fulfilled life. They usually have some good idea of what needs to happen in order that they should be happy. We decide that the achievement of a particular goal will bring about happiness and the anticipation of that outcome motivates us to act in order to bring it about. We are all actually looking for the same thing – happiness. At least, this is what Aristotle said and it seems very reasonable.

However, there will have been for all of us many things in our lives that we wanted. In some cases, we may well have been aware at the time that it was only a passing fancy, that it really did not matter very much whether or not the desire was satisfied. For others, though, it may have seemed almost a matter of life or death; that it was absolutely vital that what was wanted came about. In these situations, was it found that, if the endeavor succeeded, the result was and remained the only thing that we wanted out of life? If it failed, did our lives effectively end at that moment? Is it not the case that, regardless of whether any particular desire is obtained, we simply move on to wanting something else sooner or later? Is it possible, then, that there is some sort of *ultimate* need which, once satisfied, will really bring total fulfillment?

It is unlikely that any fulfillment will last until our death. And could one remain totally content, because of some past achievement, knowing that death was imminent? What do we mean by imminent anyway? No one lives forever. Death seems to be the ultimate and unavoidable dampener on all our ideas of lasting happiness. It brings to an end all opportunities for accomplishing any imagined purpose in our lives and renders our past and present achievements meaningless. Death effectively nullifies our existence. Subsequently, it is as if we had never been – and what could be more of a downer for the ego than that?

What aspect of ourselves is it that needs to be gratified? We have many enjoyments in life – food, possessions, friends. We like our bodies to be healthy. We want to be confident and without fears. We value intelligence and creativity. Are all of these aspects equally important? What is their relationship to us? What is our real nature, anyway? Who exactly am I? Is it simply a matter of genes?

Are we driven by our genes?

At a very basic level, are we genetically programmed to be predisposed towards some things rather than others and therefore actively to seek them out? We have evolved from apes and moved through a prolonged stage of hunter-gatherer status. Those members who survived the hardships of this sort of life were the ones whose genes favored this lifestyle. Physical adaptations such as color vision became endemic (useful for identifying flowering shrubs from a distance for example, so as to be able to see where fruit might be found subsequently).

More subtle aspects might be preference for those habitats that provide the combinations of characteristics most likely to support survival, e.g. abundance of wildlife and vegetation for food; high ground with good visibility into the distance to detect potential dangers; trees or caves etc. to provide cover and protection and so on. Thus it is that landscapes such as these are the ones that we find most attractive even today when those factors are no longer relevant for our peace of mind. To an extent almost certainly far greater than we can ever realize, our likes and dislikes and therefore our desires and fears are driven by evolutionary factors rather than personal choice.

It is often claimed that the partners that people choose are subconsciously motivated by considerations of parenthood. We prefer attractive partners because they are more likely to be healthy and pass on quality genes, young and fit ones because they will be able to find food, protect the children and so on. Many other species display those characteristics sought by potential partners as part of their behavior prior to mating and those that appear to possess these traits to the greatest extent are the ones chosen preferentially.

Even emotions might be genetically programmed. Perhaps we ought not to rely upon them at all in deciding how to act. If in saying that "I want x", I actually mean that I have a desire or fear or other emotion that seems to be pointing towards x, then perhaps I should try to ignore it altogether in any decision I make. Sartre, the French existentialist philosopher, believed that our emotions are an unconscious process. If I am afraid of something, it means that I have already assessed the situation and decided that there is a danger – hence the fear. No doubt the evolutionary psychologists would agree with this too. The fear serves the evolutionary purpose of making us extra alert and being prepared to run away. People who exhibit such a trait have survived on balance while those lacking it have not and hence the gene for this emotion has been passed on.

Throughout the animal kingdom, species evolve strategies to maximize the probability that they will pass on their genetic code to the next generation. Dragonflies will guard the female after mating until the eggs have been laid to guarantee that no other male competes with his sperm. Whales will flush out the female with large volumes of their own semen to achieve the same effect. Without any conscious decision, many animals will act in such a way as to make the only sort of mark that they can on the future, ensuring that they have not lived their lives in vain.

We do not usually become consciously aware of a need to pass on our genes, or at least not in these terms. The idea of a family dying out, if there are no males to continue the name, does still sometimes seem important, however. And, for many couples having problems conceiving a child, the need may become very important indeed. For those who lack the education to excel in intellectual spheres, the aesthetic sensibilities to be a gifted artist or musician, or the physical prowess to be a talented sportsman, this may be their only route to fame. If you are unable to realize your ambitions yourself, it might be possible through your children. Celebrity by proxy is better than anonymous death.

Irrespective of any subconscious biological drive, we are still likely to look for meaning in our lives through our children, especially in the context of a marriage. And, if unable to have genetic children, there is still a sense of purpose and fulfillment to be found in bringing up an adopted child. The genetic element seems inescapable and it is not entirely surprising that some psychologists attempt to explain away all of our behavior in these terms. They are wrong but more investigation is needed before this becomes clear.

The need for effect

The apparent drive to have some impact on their surroundings, to be able to see that their existence has had some effect, must surely be behind some of the apparently motiveless assassinations of key figures that have taken place. It as though it is felt that the fame and perceived importance of the victim will rub off on the killer. Even though the murderer may be reviled thereafter, he will at least not be forgotten. And such people have their own moment of notoriety in the eyes of the world, even if they are no longer free to enjoy it subsequently.

It is the need to feel that, once you have gone, and the small circle of friends and family have forgotten you or have themselves died, it will not simply be as though you had never existed at all. There is something quite intolerable in the thought that there might be no effective trace that we were ever here. Even if others are unaware of our impact, it can still matter that we have left our mark.

I was walking in the New Forest recently with my wife. There had been considerable rain earlier and it was very wet, to the extent that freely flowing water was visible in some places that are usually dry. My wife walked out into the middle of one of these streams and began with her boot to clear away some of the debris that was blocking the flow. She casually remarked that the flow might be the beginning of a new river and that her action could be changing the direction of flow for the future. Though most unlikely, the idea illustrates a basic instinct. It also highlights, however, the fragility and ultimate irrelevance of anything that we might do. In the case of the stream, any action short of bringing in mechanical excavators would have little effect. The stream will dry up until the next heavy rain, which will then make its own, new pathway through the valley. Even were we to use heavy equipment and construct deep channels, this would only last for decades, generations or centuries.

All man-made endeavors are doomed, swamped by longer term, natural effects. We have a map of the New Forest that is about thirty years old and it shows a track and footbridge across a particular area near where we live. In actuality, however, this is now impassable, being covered by dangerous bogs, the footbridge long ago dismantled or disintegrated.

Mountains explode, earthquakes flatten the landscape and the implacable sea tirelessly erodes our coastline. We have only been on this earth for a tiny fraction of its existence. The earth's lifetime is infinitesimal in cosmic terms. Looking at things in timescales relative to the universe rather than to our meager existence, it can be seen that nothing *really* matters at all.

But, being the egotistical, self-centered beings that we are, this wider picture is of little consequence. If our family is starving, we will cut down the rainforest to clear ground to build somewhere to live and to grow food. The longer term repercussions of this for the environment and future generations are academic. There is more than a little irony here. We are striving to do something to leave our mark on the world, so that a part of us will somehow continue into the future and, quite incidentally, we as a race are doing exactly that without specifically intending to. (Though whether our future generations will be able to flourish in the world we leave them is debatable!)

Fame and achievement

In our day to day lives, we have a basic need to feel worthwhile, both in a social context and in the workplace. And we would like to distinguish ourselves in order to stand out from the monotonous and commonplace. It is as though we need constant recognition to reassure us that we are still alive. This attitude can be seen by flicking through the pages of the *Guinness Book of Records* to see the variety of quite ludicrous activities people perform in order to be registered as the record holder, whether it is swallowing the largest number of raw eggs or staying for the longest time at the top of a flagpole. Presumably these dubious achievements do not actually make them feel in some way superior to everyone else but they clearly satisfy some perceived need, perhaps simply the acknowledgement by others of their existence.

Possibly the greatest endeavor is to achieve world-wide recognition and prominence, acceptance as the best in one's chosen sphere of activity. If this is an area approved by a large number of people, then it is clearly of far greater significance than building the highest tower of dominoes. Unfortunately, relatively few people are able to do this. Nevertheless, we can still formulate some such ambition and work towards it for much of our lives. Ironically, we can usually remain secure in the knowledge that it is likely to remain in the future as an almost abstract, rather than a tangible goal. "I, too, will be famous... one day." But, for some, goals may actually be achieved. An example that I encountered on a TV program recently was from David Gilmore of the rock band Pink Floyd. He was discussing one of the greatest pop albums of all time, *Dark Side of the Moon*, which was in the top-selling album charts for fourteen years.

He explained how his ambition had always been to become rich and famous and that this was fine whilst it remained a distant target, something to work towards. When he realized that this had actually been achieved, he was forced to reassess his situation and ask himself what it meant. He was still susceptible to all of the daily ups and downs of life, sometimes happy, sometimes miserable. Essentially he had not actually changed. There was no sense of final fulfillment. He was now being forced to ask himself "What next?" and there was no satisfactory answer. In such a situation, one is forced to concede that the achieving of such an ambition was not the solution after all.

Another example is that of Leonard Nimoy – famous as Spock in the TV series *Star Trek*. Following on from his success there, he went on to direct his own films. But then, he says, he woke up one morning thinking "Work's great. I've achieved far more that I ever thought I would achieve. But I don't feel there's anything to get up for". Shortly after this he became an alcoholic and eventually contemplated suicide.

People who come genuinely to believe in a particular cause, whether religious, environmental, social or whatever, can easily set themselves a related goal. They might want to campaign for a new law, stop a bypass being built or any key issue in the area of their concern. Whilst working towards this, they have a clear purpose to their lives. Their attention becomes positively directed towards a specific end and extraneous matters such as personal comfort, time and money can easily be ignored. The expression "single-minded" is no accident. Irrespective of the intrinsic value of their cause as far as others are concerned, the goal becomes meaningful for this person for the duration of their commitment. *Any* goal that is taken seriously can serve this function, although the more effort that is invested, the greater the sense of meaning is likely to be.

The danger is that, once the goal has been achieved, if it is not immediately superseded by a new one, it may be seen to have been a delusion. Although there may be a sense of satisfaction on completion, the sense of purpose may now be lost. Some people choose to avoid this danger by pursuing a goal that is most unlikely to be achieved but which is perceived as having value regardless. An example might be campaigning for recognition, support, money, research etc. into a rare disease. Quite probably this will be a disease that the person had never heard of... until their child died from it. Then, perhaps as an initial diversion from their grief or in an attempt to justify the death, they can "happily" devote the rest of their life to setting up and managing a charity, say, in support of other sufferers.

Fame of any sort does not usually last much beyond death. The films of a star may continue to be enjoyed for generations but few will know anything of the real person behind the roles played. How many will have read their biography? And how true will such a biography be anyway, having been written with probably deliberate sensationalism in order to sell? None of this will matter to the onetime celebrity anyway since he or she no longer exists. The need for effect does not survive death.

I have suggested that only people who are not *involved* worry about life and meaning. You may judge the truth of this from your own situation. If you are (still) reading this book, you have clearly found the time to do so. Presumably you would not have picked it up in the first place, and would certainly not have bought it, unless you are actively thinking about purpose and priority in your own life. You must be disillusioned, to some degree at least, with the projects in your life even if you are not actually suffering the excesses of existential angst described above. What do *you* want out of life?

People generally have a good idea of their long-term aims. But does achieving our goals bring lasting happiness? In fact it has been found that we soon adjust to any new condition and return our normal level of satisfaction. Another aspect is that, no matter how satisfied we might have been in an absolute sense with our life, we have an unfortunate tendency to compare this with others at or slightly above our station. It might be called the "keeping up with the Jones' syndrome".

It has been observed that x might initially be very happy when she is promoted at work and given a higher salary. But if an associate y is later promoted and given an even higher salary, then x is likely to be very *un*happy. In this situation, what I really want is not more money *per se* but more money than my peers. It is no doubt a similar principle that makes many people read or listen to so much overtly depressing news about accidents and crimes. Television series about real-life events in hospitals, watching the police investigating murders, rapists and pedophiles, people coping with illnesses or bereavement, natural disasters and so on seem to be proliferating. That the bad things have happened to someone else and not to me provides a minor fillip in a world where I might feel that I have not much to be happy about. Myers (Ref. 41) quotes the wonderful Persian saying: "I cried because I had no shoes, until I met a man who had no feet."

Feelings of achievement at work are usually reserved for those with careers and here it is often speed of promotion, size of salary, numbers of clients or whatever that is important rather than the actual work. Success is gauged by comparison with peers or with other companies, by price of shares or size of contracts. "I am better than you." Those who find themselves in such a situation can easily be sucked into the never ending race to maintain and improve the statistics, working ridiculous hours, going without exercise or meals, losing sleep.

Nevertheless, much work is challenging and offers scope for creativity and ingenuity. Retaining control of the workload, mentally balancing all of the factors, making decisions that are later seen to have been the correct ones etc. can clearly provide considerable satisfaction, within its own context at least. The sense of being competent is gratifying to the ego, as are success, esteem and material acquisitions. Whilst involved, the sense of both meaning and purpose can be strong. If there is significant interaction with clients or others, it can even be seen as an opportunity for self-expression.

Ultimately, however, all ego-related activities fail to deliver the goods. It is somewhat akin to playing a game. Whilst winning, it may seem fulfilling but after it is over, it is seen for what it always was – merely a game. When the career is brought to a halt by retirement or redundancy, the downfall can be severe indeed. There is nothing lasting to show for all of one's efforts and even one's existence is quickly forgotten by those who are left at the workplace.

If "what I want" is just an idea then, if I get it, all that is going to be satisfied is this idea. And ideas are temporary things only, coming and going with terrifying rapidity. No idea is going to provide lasting satisfaction. What we truly are deserves much more than this.

The Economist

4. The things that we want and need

So, having recognized that there are two aspects to a fulfilling life – a succession of meaningful experiences to fill our days and an overall purpose to work towards – what specific things do we actually look for to satisfy these requirements? There is a whole range from the most basic, such as food, up to the most abstract such as following the will of God. We need to look more closely at all of these and determine their relative merits in respect of our twin aims.

Our perceived needs

There are various ways of looking at and categorizing the things that we actually need in life. The system devised by psychologist Abraham Maslow is a well known one and as good as any. He argued that our behavior is driven by our needs and that these have to be satisfied according to a fundamental sequence. We are not going to worry about going to concerts and art galleries if we haven't eaten for several days. The most basic necessities are food, water and clothing. If the body is not comfortable, we will not, in general, be able to direct it towards other goals.

Next comes the requirement for shelter and some degree of security. We want to know that we have a metaphorical cave to which we can retreat when life becomes difficult; a wall to stand against when threatened or a fire to keep the wild animals at bay. We want to feel safe, comfortable and secure or at least know that we are able to be so at the end of a day's excitement and escapism. The latter are all very well in small doses but people whose days and nights are spent looking around for potential enemies and worrying where and when the next danger is going to arrive end up with stress disorders.

Nowadays, we might tend to think that those who strive only to maintain a sense of coziness are somehow missing out on what life is all about. The philosopher Nietzsche, for example, had nothing but contempt for those who prized comfort and security above all else; he thought this emblematic of the middle-class British mentality. But security is nevertheless justifiably one of Maslow's basic needs since, until we are assured of our survival from one moment to the next, we cannot devote much effort to our ultimate aim of achieving happiness. Associated with this, perhaps from an evolutionary sense, is our drive to be with others, whether as just another member of a social gathering or as a close friend of one or two others. It is obvious from the TV wildlife programs that animals are safest when in a group. There is more chance of spotting and evading potential predators and, if one should attack anyway, there is a smaller chance of being the victim. It is therefore inevitable that those genes that predispose their owners to be happy in such situations will be selected preferentially over time.

But we cannot always be secure. If early man had spent all his time in the security of the cave and not sometimes ventured out, risking his life to catch a woolly mammoth for lunch, we might not be here today. In order to move forward and evolve, in all of the ways that that concept entails, we have to seek out new challenges and boldly split new infinitives. (Apologies to those who have never seen the TV series *Star Trek*. The now-famous line from the introduction has the heroes "seeking out new life forms, to boldly go where no man has gone before.") Man as a species would not have attained such dominance in the world had he not had this irresistible urge to move forever forward into new territory and find new experiences. Having established a secure home to which we can return when life becomes too uncertain, we look to expand our range of experiences. We want to move to a larger house, take a year's sabbatical and travel the world, emigrate or even journey to the moon, in spirit if not bodily. It is interesting that one of the first personality-related genes identified in the human genome project was one deemed responsible for risk-taking (and, interestingly, this was also linked to a predisposition for taking drugs).

The "physiological" and "safety" levels of need provide us with our basic survival and comfort. Once these desires have been satisfied, we can move on to higher social and ideological motivations. The first of these, according to Maslow, is the innate desire to belong to a group, being accepted by them and feeling the bonds of friendship and love. He called this the "Social" or "Affection" level.

The first group of "others" consists of our relations, those with whom we initially interact irrespective of choice. Our parents and siblings are the inner circle, introducing us to language and shaping our thoughts and desires. It is through them that we gain recognition of ourselves as individuals. We are dependent upon them for food and shelter and they provide our introduction to social intercourse. In societies such as that in Japan, children remain strongly influenced by their families and the drive to become independent is absent.

No one wants to feel isolated and alone; we naturally seek out the company and affection of others, moving out from family to form friends, then looking for special friends and perhaps seeking to build a new family. To some degree we look for friendship with those who share our own interests but it is also inevitable that we will be influenced by the ideas of others and find ourselves investing energy in new endeavors.

Maslow's next level is called "Esteem" or 'Status" – the recognition by others of our worth as a person in our chosen profession, sport or hobby. Without such appreciation, we are unable to achieve a satisfactory level of self-esteem, feeling that we are fulfilling a useful role in life. People differ in the degree to which they think they need this. Many strong-minded individuals are happy to do what they themselves want, irrespective of what others might think but most of us seem to have a basic need to feel that we are thought well of by others and that, when we achieve something, others will take notice and approve.

And we like to be liked by others – if not actually admired, at least thought of as someone who is worthy of being regarded as a friend. Psychological studies have shown that those who feel that they are liked and respected by their family and associates are healthier and report being happier. When this feeling is absent, it is interesting to note that people often seem to prefer to be hated or reviled rather than being ignored altogether. Rather be remembered as a bully or criminal than pass through life and into death completely unnoticed.

The final level of Maslow's hierarchy, which becomes relevant once all of the lower requirements have been adequately met, is what he called "Self-actualization." This he understood as realizing our potential in whichever area might be most relevant to our particular nature. As an example, irrespective of what our employment might be, we might feel that what we really ought to be doing is painting. We might pursue this half-heartedly as a hobby but, if we finally abandon our job and devote ourselves entirely to this pursuit and ultimately achieve recognition as a great artist, then we would have become self-actualized.

We have occasional premonitions of this final state in what he called "peak experiences." In these we feel truly alive. They contain all of the most positive elements that we encounter in such states as involvement, excitement, moments of achievement and so on. There is no desire, no sense of lack but instead a feeling that we are truly ourselves, fulfilled and wanting for nothing. Everything is simple and natural, effortless and spontaneous. The moment is full of meaning – and significantly empty of ego.

Maslow's hierarchy sounds very reasonable and most would probably agree with it in a general sense. Nevertheless, there are some who dispense with a home and its associated security in order to travel the world, for example. It used to be a traditional phase of man's spiritual development in India that, after he had been educated and had raised a family, a man would go to live in the forest to complete his studies prior to renouncing everything. In this final phase, he would live out the remainder of his life entirely reliant upon the charity of others for food and clothing, living outdoors and spending his time in meditation. Clearly for such a person, even the most basic needs have ceased to become a cause for concern. Even amongst ordinary people today, there are many who are prepared to take risks, even to the extent of losing their home, in order to realize their ambitions.

We can certainly appreciate that it may not be possible to be happy unless our basic needs are satisfied. We need to be healthy with a source of food for the foreseeable future and a roof over our heads before we can think about what we want to do with our lives in order to feel fulfilled. But, though the essence of the theory may fit well with most people, there are sufficient exceptions to suggest that Maslow was missing something fundamental. Long term prisoners in terrible conditions, fearing for their lives can experience moments of intense happiness. People who suddenly become blind or paralyzed can find positive meaning and purpose to their lives when this had previously been absent. In such cases, the suffering seems to *prompt* such people into looking for meaning in order to rationalize their experience, whereas previously they had had no cause to think about it. Thus it is that material and physical needs *may* be relevant but they are not necessarily so.

Another problem with Maslow's theory is that he stopped at the level of fulfilling our potential in our chosen field of activity. But, as we saw with David Gilmore and Leonard Nimoy, this is not necessarily enough. Most of us, of course, can always see further development of our abilities stretching into the future, whether this be promotion to managing director or writer of a Nobel prize winning, best selling book of all time. There are very few who reach the top and then, looking back, are able to ask whether it was worth it.

Perhaps it is simply the case that none of us really knows what we want, or even who we really are. And perhaps this ignorance is our basic problem, even though it is too close at hand to recognize. To resolve the problem would then be a missing level of achievement, which has to be higher than Maslow's self-actualization. The achievement here is to find out just who we really are, beyond mere accomplishment or recognition. Such a level of achievement is called "Enlightenment" or "Self-realization." It has acquired mystical overtones ever since the terms became generally acknowledged in the west, probably following the popularization of transcendental meditation in the nineteen sixties. It is not mystical, nor need it be viewed in the traditional religious manner. The problem is that our way of thinking is so habitual, and our sense of ego so deep-rooted, that it is difficult to talk about in terms that do not trigger antipathy or disbelief. Accordingly, the topic has to be approached circumspectly!

So, let's return to look more closely at the things that we typically believe that we want or need in order to be happy. If we analyze them more carefully, we may be able to see why they will never bring happiness and perhaps, thereby, gain some insight into what really matters.

Health and fitness

If you look in a thesaurus, you may be surprised at how many positive-sounding phrases are associated with being healthy. And, if you are chronically ill or have experienced a prolonged period of illness or a serious accident, you will know how everything else seems to become insignificant. We say: "*I* am not feeling well." What we are really talking about, of course, is the *body* not being healthy. The extent to which we associate the state of our body with whether or not we feel happy or fulfilled is a measure of how completely most of us believe that we *are* our bodies.

There is no denying that it seems *very* important to most of us that we are healthy; that we eat good food and do not become over-weight; that we visit the dentist regularly and check that we don't have lumps in any of the places that ought not to have them. We could draw an analogy with looking after a car. If it is to be maintained in good running condition, we must ensure that the engine is regularly checked by a good mechanic and we don't let the brake fluid run dry. And, most importantly, we must keep it supplied with petrol. If significant parts, such as a wheel, become damaged, these will have to be fixed or replaced.

I may feel it desirable that the bodywork is kept clean and shiny but now we have moved out of the realm of actual needs. I just realized this morning, for example, that the aerial on my car is missing, probably removed by vandals to play with for a few minutes and then throw away. I could have reacted with a cry of horror that *my* car had been violated. Fortunately, there was only a minor feeling of annoyance that the radio would probably not now receive a sufficiently good signal and the realization that here was yet another call on my virtually non-existent income.

Of course, we should take care of our bodies. If we don't eat and look after them when they are ill, then they are likely to deteriorate and we may not be around long enough to be able to find out what really matters in life. But, to continue with the metaphor, it is important that the car is in good working condition so that we can drive it to where we want to go. The functioning of the engine etc. is not an end itself. It may boost the ego to have it standing outside the house all day looking as though it has just been wheeled out of the showroom but it is missing the point altogether if we do not actually use it.

But we have to keep remembering that, when I ask the question "What do I need", the answer will depend upon who I think I am. If I answer that *I* really need to keep healthy – and there is actually a common saying to the effect that the most important thing in your life is your health – that presupposes that I actually *am* the body. By all means admit that it is important that we look after the body but, even if you do not actually phrase it in this way, this is how we should think of it. There is no question but that I appear to rely on this body in many ways. It is through its senses that I am aware of the world outside. If the body is not maintained in good working condition, through judicious application of nutritious food, water etc. and appropriate treatment whenever something ceases to function correctly, then it will not continue to provide for my real needs, assuming that there are some to be discovered.

Fashion

It is worth pursuing the metaphor of the car and its body just a little further because most of us seem to have been conned by the fashion industry into believing that "looking after our bodywork" *is* very important. "I need a new dress so that I can go to the party next week" is surely equivalent to saying "I can't possibly drive anywhere until I've polished the car". Although one might initially think in this way, a little reflection will show that this is an idea founded on vanity. What is almost certainly the case is that no one will notice (or care) that you are wearing the same dress that you wore when you went to Kathy's party last year. Indeed, the only people who might conceivably think like this will be concerned about what everyone else thinks of *them* rather than paying any attention to what you are wearing.

OK, this is over-simplifying the situation because I have not taken due cognizance of this thing called fashion and that, of course, is how the industry functions. If that dress I wear should be the wrong color, length, material or whatever as compared with what is considered current fashion, then fashionable people may well notice. They have been taken in by the media forces and genuinely believe that they will be thought somehow inferior or at least sadly out of touch if they have not thrown their money away on the latest gear, even though their existing wardrobe has hardly been worn.

And this is actually how it operates for many people. Children are ridiculed and victimized at school because they are not wearing the latest style of trainers. Teenagers spend most of their income keeping up with trends that are forever rushing on ahead of them. Even people who do actually acknowledge that they are being manipulated in this way give in to the pressure less they are thought ill of by their peers.

In more reflective moments, we might admit that we don't actually need up to date clothes. As long as we have warm, water-proof clothes for the winter and cool, light ones for the summer, we need not pay any attention to what the current magazines and TV adverts try to tell us that we must have.

The excesses of succumbing to the pressure of advertising and wanting to be fashionable can be very serious. We all know that children are maturing more quickly these days (or certainly think they are!). It is now the case that girls as young as seven or eight are becoming dangerously concerned about their bodies. Not only do they pester their parents for the latest designs but they actually seek to wear clothes to project a "sexy" image. Many wear make up and high-heeled shoes. And, if this were not bad enough, some girls who are already underweight, begin to diet, copying their mothers or other role models. It is hardly surprising that increasing numbers of teenagers are becoming anorexic, their attitudes shaped and manipulated by the media and peers so that they no longer have conscious control of such basic functions as eating when hungry.

And the ideas behind this behavior are self-propagating. Primary school children, filling out a questionnaire on the subject, believe that slim children are attractive and vivacious while fat children are ugly, lazy and smelly. They grow up passing these attitudes on to others and ultimately to their own children. Such ideas are also self-fulfilling to some degree. The fat children believe they are inadequate and fail to exercise or eat less, no doubt deriving some comfort from their over-eating. Consequently they remain trapped in this scenario and are very likely to fail on other fronts too. Advertising has a lot to answer for! And it is not simply in the realm of clothes…

Materialism

"Today you're unhappy? Can't figure it out? Go shopping!" This quote is the playwright Arthur Miller's cynical solution to finding happiness. When I discovered that my wife's sister-in-law and her children were intending to go on holiday to the US, I wondered which aspects might be enticing them. I have never been myself and would very much like to see the city of San Francisco, the scenery of Yosemite and the Grand Canyon to begin with. I would probably even find a visit to Cape Canaveral and Disneyland interesting, though these would be some way down the list. I was, I think the appropriate phrase is "gob smacked" however, when I asked my teenaged niece why she wanted to go to America and she answered: "the shops"! It seems to me to be one of the principal indictments of Western society that these are the values being inculcated in young people through the media – the cult of materialism and desiring possessions.

Our perceived needs will always be relative to our environment, upbringing and education. Most of us are unlikely ever to have to worry about where our next meal will come from or where we will sleep tonight. We take for granted many items that were once considered luxuries and only appreciate their value if they are stolen or break down. Domestic accessories such as refrigerators, electric kettles and toasters, entertainment sources such as television, CD players, computers and mobile phones are all used daily without a thought. We would be unlikely to claim that they are all really necessary yet we may still feel deprived if forced to manage without them. But there are many places in the world where such items are rare. In much of Afghanistan for example, there is no electricity so that most of the above are somewhat redundant. To those people, then, there can be no question of necessity regarding much that we consider essential – you can always manage without something you have never had.

The materially minded West is responsible for much of our unrest by inculcating in us the perceived need (i.e. desire) for so many things and the consequent investment of much of our time and effort into obtaining them. We always tend to move in circles of like-minded people so that, if this is what matters to us, we will be able to compare our material standing with our peers. If we think that we are falling behind, a feeling of dissatisfaction is almost inevitable. The fight to work harder, to earn more money in order to keep up with them, is then probably going to worsen the situation still more. At the extreme, which is often seen in prestigious jobs such as stock broking in the financial sector of any major city, people can end up with masses of money but no time to spend it. Marriages break up and health suffers. Where is the happiness in any of this?

Today's attitudes seem to be molded by commercial advertising in one form or another. We are persuaded that we must have the latest model or the newest accessory; advances in technology make faultlessly functioning equipment obsolete. Not only must we throw away our expensive record players but all of the LPs lovingly acquired over the years suddenly become superfluous. Computers are evolving so quickly that any new model becomes outdated in less than three years. This evolutionary process is now necessary to sustain both the manufacturers themselves and the economy of the country. Marketing departments work overtime trying to think of extra knobs and minor variations that will persuade the consumers to purchase the latest version until the next generation comes along. And these are quite likely to be less reliable and may not even perform the basic functions as well as the old model.

Many people spend much of their free time (and most of their spare cash) buying almost for the sake of it. Shopping has become an addiction – a disease cultivated by the manufacturers and propagated by the media. We can even shop in bed now, using our laptops connected to the Internet. Some people actually have to resort to drugs to cure the illness. I had thought that the word "shopaholic" was a pun but it is deadly serious. An estimated one million people in the UK and five million in the US are sufferers and anti-depressant drugs are prescribed by understanding doctors. Yet it does not seem that this addiction is driven by a need for the goods themselves – these often end up unused in a bottom drawer a few weeks later; it is the act of satisfying the desire that provides the payoff.

Surveys have shown that, while our desire for material goods increases as our incomes increase, our overall happiness decreases. Tim Kasser, who conducted one such study in Illinois, believes that governments should put a health warning on advertising. Materialism seems to bring about principally negative effects for the consumer – both mental and physical. The ones who benefit are the manufacturers, the advertising bureaus, the media and the government (through taxation and maintenance of the economy). This last one is our only gain, a needful one admittedly in the context of a materially based society.

We are constantly coerced into desiring each innovation and committing ourselves to months of overtime in order to scrape together the money to buy it. Are we really so gullible? Unfortunately, yes! But that is not actually the point of this discussion. If it were really true that, having saved the money and bought the item in question, we were actually made happy as a result, then perhaps it would all be justifiable. But of course this never happens. For a short time, we may feel a sense of relief and achievement (smug satisfaction?) but this does not last. We may well derive enjoyment from the purchase in question but this quickly wears off too. All too soon, the passing of time means that we are now used to having the object. It is no longer a novelty; in fact, much though we may prefer it were not so, it might even be becoming outdated or worse still, tasteless.

The other influential factor is whether our friend or neighbor has the object in question while we do not. Envy is another emotion subtly promoted by advertisers. If she has one and I don't, I feel somehow cheated. If only I could have one too, then I would be happy. I would be even happier if I could be the first in my circle of acquaintances to have one. After all, if everyone has got one, there is no novelty value and no one is going to be envious of *me*.

We know all of this and, when it is put so bluntly, we would freely admit that it is more than a little pathetic. Why, then, are we repeatedly taken in by the deception? What is going on in our minds to cause us to act in this way? Well, it shouldn't be surprising at all. We have heard of the lottery winners whose lives go to pieces when they suddenly become rich. The lives of the famous rarely seem to run smooth – film stars divorce and remarry more frequently than some people take holidays. Millionaires may even commit suicide. Getting what you think you want does not seem to be the answer. As George Bernard Shaw said: *"There are two tragedies in life. One is not to get your heart's desire. The other is to get it"*.

Happiness obviously does not exist in objects but neither is it to be found through the acquisition of them. In fact, it has nothing to do with objects at all but in the satisfaction of our desire for them. This is a key point and will explain much when we look at happiness in more detail in the next chapter.

Living for the moment

Another one of my relatives apparently had a very promising future while at school. By his last year he had become head boy, being both popular and clever. He played chess for the town team. We all expected him to go to university to study law or something equally prestigious and work towards an intellectually and financially rewarding career. What actually happened is that he left school without applying for any university and eventually joined a company that provides contract laborers, traveling around the country to do purely manual work in the building trade.

What is going on in a situation such as this? Clearly his perceived needs, whatever they might have been, were not seen as being satisfied by prolonging his academic involvement, by learning more and having to spend further years without any income. He saw his less academic friends already earning money, going out drinking and clubbing, and did not want to be left out. The satisfaction of the relatively limited needs of pleasure and entertainment seemingly overrode any longer term ideals of highly paid and satisfying career. He claims to be happy but one cannot help wondering whether there will be regret in later years, if not sooner. Such pleasures, being of an intrinsically transient nature, must ultimately be seen as shallow. Inevitably, as we grow older, we feel that we need to search for something that is more lasting.

Of course, the materialistic outlook is the one promoted by the media. They try to persuade us that such pleasures are the ones that bring the most satisfaction. You must have money in order to be happy and if you have to wait three or more years before you can even begin to earn any, the world might be over, ravaged by plague spread by terrorists. If someone is not prepared to appraise such a philosophy sincerely and seriously, how are we to persuade them otherwise? They have the immediate feedback of their senses. One path brings pleasure, the other apparently endless months and years of hard work, learning useless facts and having few outlets for interim reward. One path satisfies your current desires, at least to some degree, while the other postpones them all into a very uncertain future. At a superficial level, how can there be any doubt about which course of action to follow?

In a situation such as this, it is as though we are weighing up all

of the factors and trying to optimize the outcome. We are prepared
to put up with a mundane job that provides an income sufficient to
cater for our entertainment. The boredom of the work is balanced
against such things as lack of stress and not having the prerequisite
of having to spend several years of hard study to obtain qualifica-
tions. The resulting salary may only provide for a second hand
family car instead of new sports model and so on. But, if one's
pleasures are relatively simple and ambitions are limited in scope,
then the consideration of all the factors may result in a logical
decision *not* to aim for a high powered job. This sort of analysis
even has a name – the "hedonic calculus". Hedonism is the philosophy of pursuing pleasure as the primary aim in life. The idea
behind the hedonic calculus is that we quantify and add up all of
the factors to decide how the result will impact on our overall
enjoyment, maximizing the happiness and minimizing the pain.

Involvement

Recalling again the Pathetique mood that I described at the
beginning of the section on Meaning, you will remember that I
used to think that *involvement* was the tool that people used to
avoid coming face to face with the reality of despair. I want to
differentiate involvement from *pleasure* and *happiness* (which
have their own section next), though it does contain elements of
both. It is closely allied with the giving of attention and the lack of
distraction from anything else.

We have five senses and we have thinking and feeling. These
constitute the objects of our consciousness. Normally, no single
one of these operates to the exclusion of all others; we are
potentially able to direct our attention to whatever is deemed to be

most worthy. Usually, this will be dictated by habit. If interested in cars, our eyes will be drawn to a rare model passing us on the road. If we are interested in models of a different kind, a short skirt passing in the street might distract us. At such moments, our normal, relatively wide attention narrows down to something much smaller. If some sudden noise or other sensation is received, the attention becomes single-pointed and everything else is momentarily excluded from our awareness.

You might be watching television when a squealing of tyres sounds outside of the house. For a moment, you become quite unaware of what is showing on the screen as your attention is taken away and, in all probability, you wait with dread for the sound of a possible crash. While the squealing sound lasts, there are no other thoughts or sensations. Normally, although supposedly we may be concentrating on one thing, there are many other peripheral sensations that partially cloud the clarity. We rarely experience this sharpness voluntarily.

Note that involvement can take different forms. In the example above, we might have said that we were "involved" in the TV program before the car braked. The nature of that experience is comparable to day dreaming. In fact, recent psychological experiments suggest that the viewer is frequently half asleep. Again we are not conscious of ourselves *doing* anything – the watching takes place automatically. This "forgetting ourselves" is key to the enjoyment of these activities; off in an imagined other world where more exciting things happen. But it is unreal and thus ultimately unsatisfying. If we are unable to find true satisfaction in the world, we may well choose to spend as much time as possible in these worlds of the imagination – this, after all is the attraction of drugs.

But contrast the experience of watching the TV with that of the alert awareness of the squealing brakes – now you are alive again!

Another characteristic of happiness or fulfillment in activity is the obtaining of positive feedback during the action. If we decide to do something in the expectation of a specific benefit and experience only negative feelings with no sign of the anticipated reward, then we are likely to abandon the attempt. What typically happens in an activity that we particularly enjoy is that in the beginning we perform poorly. As time goes on, however, we learn a little, discover that we are able to do something that we could not initially do and this provides us with a fillip and the incentive to continue and learn a bit more. In a really fulfilling activity, there seems to be an unending scope for this improvement so that we are always being provided with renewed enthusiasm through repeated positive feedback.

Sport is a good example of activities which can be performed for their own sake rather than because some particular outcome is desired – even when we lose we can still find them enjoyable, providing that we feel that we have performed as well as we were able and did not do anything silly. In fact, players of competitive sport often seek to play against opponents who are known to be more skilled. They know in advance that they will almost certainly lose but also believe that it is only by taking on more challenging opposition that they can improve their own performance. It is a case of constantly exposing themselves to increasing challenges as their skills increase. The two have to be balanced so that they neither feel too inadequate in the face of vastly superior opposition nor so skilled that they are wasting their time. Those who are already so good that they are unable to find any opponents to give them a good game are forever playing below their best and are very likely to become bored. Also, if we play solely to win, the simple enjoyment of the activity for its own sake is lost.

Work usually falls into the play to win category, the prize being the money that we need in order to live. It is because we are doing it only for the result that we do not usually enjoy it. In fact, when we become involved, the goal is temporarily forgotten and it does become possible simply to do the job. Providing that there are challenges commensurate with our skills and we are able to cope with any difficulties and obtain feedback as to how we are faring, enjoyment can come quite naturally.

This is another aspect of involvement and it retains its favorable and encouraging effect whilst we are taking part, anticipating, reflecting or otherwise thinking about it. But there is always the danger that, in a different context, when there is no thought relating to the sport or whatever it might be, that the ultimate shallowness will be realized and it will be seen not to be a meaningful end in itself.

Finally, you can certainly observe some very busy individuals who are nevertheless unhappy. Such people are constantly looking for things to do in order to avoid having to face up to what they perceive as the essential meaninglessness of their lives. It is the ego that thinks like this and, when we are deeply involved in an activity, the ego is forgotten and our true nature of happiness shines through. But, when we perform tasks deliberately looking for this result, the ego persists, worrying and imagining and all the rest. The real self is still obscured and we remain unhappy, though giving all the appearance of being involved.

Money

There is clearly a perceived correlation between having money and being happy. Many people cite the lack of it as being a major obstacle to happiness, even those that most of us would think of as being rich already. We tend to think that those richer than ourselves must be happier. We also naturally consider those with significantly more money than ourselves to be rich, but most people do not think of themselves as rich, no matter how much money they may have.

Studies do show, however, that those people with higher incomes tend to report being more satisfied with life than those with lower ones. Looking back to Maslow's hierarchy, it seems obvious that those unable to satisfy basic needs such as food and security are bound to be somewhat unhappy. Nevertheless, once an acceptable standard has been attained, further increases do not produce greater happiness. In fact, since the fifties, though effective income has doubled in the US, the perceived level of happiness has fallen slightly. Those who aim for material success, status and high income, report lower levels of well being than those who value friendship and marriage more highly. As the psychologist David Myers has put it (Ref. 44): *"Happiness seems less a matter of getting what we want than of wanting what we have"*.

The problem is that our attitude to material possessions adjusts according to our ability to obtain them. Suppose that some new electronic device comes onto the market and we see all of our peers seduced into buying them. Providing that the price is not too far out of our reach, it is likely that we will want one too. We will save the money (or, more likely these days, reach for the nearest credit card) and buy one for ourselves. For a time, we will feel pleased and enjoy the novelty of our new toy. But all too soon we become accustomed to having it, forget what it was like to be without it, and turn our attention to something else.

Fortunately, it works the other way round too. Before I was made redundant a number of years ago, I had a reasonably well paid job. My wife and I did not have a profligate lifestyle – we did not go on expensive holidays, follow all of the fashions in clothes or go out to clubs or expensive restaurants. But then we would occasionally go away for the weekend and think nothing about going out to see a play, buying a book or a CD. Since then, forced to live on an early pension and a few savings, we literally monitor all of our outgoings and think carefully before indulging ourselves in any way. Naturally, there is some disappointment in not being able routinely to pursue some of the activities that we used to but, overall, our level of satisfaction with life is not significantly diminished. In fact, from my own point of view, writing books is a distinct improvement upon the profession that I previously followed.

It often seems that the government bases its decisions on whatever will generate the most money. In recent years in the UK, this even seems to extend to health care, rail travel, education and social services. Nowadays many will decide to go to university so that they will get a higher paid job at the end rather than for the purpose of receiving a good education. Prior to the nineteen seventies, developing a meaningful philosophy of life was deemed to be a much more important reason for attending college. *Sic transit gloria mundi!*

Culture and creativity

Some people recognize that material goods in themselves are of little ultimate value. Fashionable items merely feed the vanity of the ego and there is no virtue in buying the most expensive unless the additional quality and durability genuinely merit the extra cost. If we forget the slogans of the advertisers, ignore the glossy brochures and the prompting of gullible friends, simply asking ourselves what we really need, we know what is reasonable.

At a higher level, there are other apparent needs, relating to the mind and intellect: the need to be mentally stimulated, the thirst for knowledge and the creative urge. Such needs themselves presuppose others being satisfied first. If you live in a city, you may after a while feel that you need to get away, perhaps go to live in the country or by the sea. Certainly this is exactly how I felt some thirty years ago, after living in London for three years. (I doubt that I could survive so long today!) After a day at the office, you probably feel a need for some peace and quiet or perhaps a gin and tonic and some relaxing classical music.

I have only recently come to appreciate the wonderful writing of Charles Dickens. I remember having to read *David Copperfield* at school but not enjoying it particularly. But then it was an abridged edition so that most of the subtleties of his writing were completely lost. Not that I would have appreciated them anyway because I was simply too inexperienced in the world, knowing little of the contemporary history or the devious ways in which people behave and so on. It is necessary to be educated in many areas and to live for many years simply in order to accumulate an understanding of life. But now, when I read "Our Mutual Friend" for example, I can enjoy it enormously, marveling at his brilliant characterizations and laughing out loud at his clever remarks, at the same time appreciating how he was condemning the government of the time for allowing the continuation of the social injustices that he portrayed.

But now we have moved out of the realm of concrete objects that can be broken or repaired. The mind is subtle and we may shy away from calling it an object. But is it also no longer mechanical, as our bodies are? In order to answer questions such as this, we need to be detached observers, not laying claim to everything that is seen or done. We naturally say "I am thinking this" or "I am doing this" and rarely consider that it might not actually be like that. We will have to look much more closely at all of these things before any reasoned conclusions can be made.

Friends and acquaintances

It was noted earlier that one of Maslow's identified needs was that of belonging to a group, both for the safety, support and security that this provides and also for the recognition by and approval of others for what we do and who we think we are. People turn to friends and family to help them to cope with the negative aspects of life, ill heath, divorce, bereavement and so on. If they have this support, they tend to recover more quickly and in general report higher levels of well-being. Those who do not have it succumb to depression or worse. Stress is a causal factor in many illnesses and any element that alleviates stress is likely to be beneficial. Close friendship is such a source. It has been found that simply having a friend or counselor, even an inexperienced one, to listen to one's troubles can be as helpful as visiting a psychotherapist or other professional. It is the fact that they are listening and offering support that counts.

It could well be the case that most people join a church simply for the sense of belonging to a community rather than because they firmly believe in a particular doctrine. This was certainly the case for my own parents who were unable to explain to me the differences between the Methodist faith and other denominations. They had joined this church simply because it happened to be the closest to our home. And the decreasing frequency of their attendance as the years went by was presumably due to the fact that they had not formed any particular friends there. My mother began to attend regularly once more in recent years because one of her few friends was also an attendee. Simply belonging to a church community and having the support of other members at times of ill health or crisis is likely significantly to affect one's general outlook and happiness.

When things are going well, people want to share their experience. Sitting on top of a mountain after an arduous climb, eating a picnic and trying to make out the landmarks in the distance is a marvelous experience – but made much more so by sharing it with another. Whether experiencing the bad or the good, if we are on our own, there is a strong tendency to be aware of this fact. It is natural to want to talk, if only to clarify the ideas in one's own mind. If we can hear sympathetic words when we are in pain, or corroborative enthusiasm during moments of enjoyment, this helps to remove the sense of isolation. The phrase "taking us out of ourselves" is a very expressive one. The involvement with others helps remove the perpetual tendency to be aware of our individuality, ideally helping us to forget the ego that is forever taking us away from the happiness that is our true nature.

Pursuing individuality as an end, only ever thinking of what *I* want, constantly reinforces the ego. This fosters an attachment to something that, as we shall see, does not in fact exist and is therefore ultimately meaningless.

As has been mentioned before, natural selection has led to our being social animals and it is therefore inevitable that we should be inclined to seek companionship even if this is no longer needed to protect us from potential predators. Lonely people tend to be unhappy and are prone to depression. Solitary confinement is still used as the ultimate form of punishment short of torture and execution. Those who seek and find friendship are happier than those who look to material gain as a source of satisfaction. In questionnaires, friendship and other close relationships are ranked higher than anything else on scales of meaningfulness. With more and more people living alone and with increased mobility making the formation of long-term friendships more difficult, it is hardly surprising that today's society is registering higher levels of unhappiness.

We tend to feel that sharing and being with others somehow makes us more complete. Feeling incomplete is a basic drive for so many of our activities. We feel that we have a fundamental lack that can only be filled by something outside. This is essentially a long-winded description of the single word *desire*. And in the same way that we feel temporary happiness and fulfillment when we obtain a long-desired object, so also we feel that basic deficiency has been removed when we form a long-term partnership for example. And that brings us on to…

Love and marriage

Love is thought by most people to be even more important than friendship, even if they are not quite sure what it is. Some eighty per cent of adults apparently believe that it is fundamental to their happiness. Studies have consistently found that married couples report higher levels of contentment than those living alone. The lowest levels are claimed by the divorced and separated, who presumably lament what they have lost.

It is perhaps not surprising that close, supportive relationships should help make life more enjoyable; sharing experiences rather than having them on one's own. Here again is the indication that those situations that take us away us from the self-centered world of ego driven desires and fears are the ones most conducive to happiness.

It used to be the case that the key ambition of most young women was to find a suitable partner, get married and raise children. This was seen as the full realization of their potential in life. As readers of Jane Austen will know, love and happiness were subsidiary factors in this; far more important was that the husband had money so that she and the children could be comfortably provided for. (Fortunately, of course, her heroines seemed to get the best of all outcomes.) A recent UK Government sponsored paper on "Life Satisfaction" (Ref. 39) investigated those aspects that seem to increase people's assessment of how happy they are. This observed that: *'studies suggest that marriage is equivalent to an increase in income of £72,000 per annum"*! On the negative side, however, those people who end up in a marriage which they deem not to be a happy one report very low levels of happiness overall, lower even than the separated or divorced.

It is interesting to note that having children has a *negative* effect on the perceived happiness of partners. The additional level of commitment may well cement the marriage but the level of happiness does not return to that of the pre-children stage until the children have left the home! This finding was not believed when reported for the first time but subsequent studies have corroborated it many times.

The compensation, and reason why people still carry on having children, is that it provides meaning. Bringing up a child, taking part in all of its discoveries, contributing to its learning, instilling values, seeing the subsequent achievements and so on are very rewarding. Children have an endless succession of needs that must be provided for by the parents and the satisfying of those needs provides continual positive feedback and a sense of value. The potential for this often increases as time goes on, with grandchildren providing still further scope. This example shows very clearly that having a sense of meaning in life and being happy are not at all the same thing.

Nowadays, many women believe, or are persuaded by peers and media, that they should expect and strive for satisfaction in all of the areas once the preserve of men. They are clearly capable of qualifying for and achieving as much if not more in many domains. Ambitious in their work, wanting to travel and experience as much as they are able, they no longer want to be tied to the home. What was once seen as the highest pursuit is now likely to be thought to be the acceptance of an end to all of their other hopes and dreams, or at least an indefinite postponement of them.

And this is all perfectly understandable. In Jane Austen's time, women were unable to pursue many of the traditional male ambitions and it was assumed by a society whose values tended to overwhelm those of the individual that their lives would revolve around the home. Now they are equally free to pursue other aims. Unfortunately, having and bringing up a child are tasks that impact far more on the woman's life than the man's so that the decision to do this is a much more serious one for them.

The whole business of love and marriage can be rationalized in the context of evolution. We feel more protective towards our family than to strangers because they share part of our genetic make-up. It is especially in our interest to look after our children because our genetic continuity is vested in them. If they themselves do not survive to have their own children then we will effectively die out. Of lower precedence is the drive to protect our brothers and sisters – they only share some of our genes (unless they are twins) – and this protective urge diminishes in proportion to the closeness of the relation. The Christian doctrine of Love Thy Neighbor is therefore never going to be followed literally. A stranger will share none of our own familial DNA, though paradoxically, of course there will be vastly more that is common than is not.

Within this context it makes evolutionary sense for partners intending to have children together to have special feelings towards each other because they are jointly investing in the future. This rationale is not usually conscious but most people acknowledge that they do not ever have a choice about falling in love – it happens outside of their control. The evolutionary psychologist Steven Pinker points out that we all want to find the optimum partner in terms of all of the attributes you might think relevant – physical attractiveness, intelligence, health, wealth etc. And we tend to end up with the best that we can find (who will also have *us*!), given that we cannot spend our whole lives looking.

If this were all there was to it however, it would not be a very secure situation, given that each of us would be highly likely to encounter someone better qualified as time went on. Whichever partner found someone better would then be likely to leave their spouse. This uncertainty would not be desirable for the loser and people would be reluctant to put all of their efforts into the relationship, knowing that it might ultimately be wasted. It is thus logical to suppose that there is effectively a gene for love, which predisposes a couple to stay together at least until the children have been raised. Such a strategy maximizes the likelihood of our genetic continuity.

Certainly people seem to fall in love without any consideration of reason. As someone once said, love is a word made up of two vowels, two consonants and two fools. They commit to the relationship because of an emotion, not because of an overt rationalization that the other person happens to be the best that they can find at the moment. It is effectively a state of intoxication and scarcely seems reasonable grounds for entering into a long-term relationship. Nevertheless, this emotion is not something that you choose to have and cannot be dropped at will. The emotional commitment confers evolutionary advantage on the species. Partners eventually form stable bonds and usually bring up children, thus propagating the love gene.

Recent research has actually proposed a specific gene that might be involved. It is responsible for constructing that part of the brain that is sensitive to a hormone called vasopressin, which is released during sex. It is also present in species other than man and the gene's length seems to be an indication of the owner's tendency to form a stable pair bond with a specific member of the opposite sex. Thus one species of vole that has a long genetic sequence in this area forms monogamous relationships while another species which lacks the gene altogether does not. It has been observed that the length varies in humans between individuals, which could explain why some people form stable relationships (i.e. fall in love) more easily than others. It is certainly true that a tendency to divorce seems to run in the family, with adopted children being more like their real parents than their foster ones (i.e. if their real parents are divorced, the children are more likely to divorce even if they did not know their real parents).

But perhaps this is all irrelevant to the matter in hand. What we are concerned with is not why we are driven to feel as we do but what we should do *given* that we feel as we do. Accepted that we do fall in love and do want to share our lives with another, what should we make of this in the grand scheme of things? Should it be relevant that the emotion is beyond our control? Certainly we cannot take the attitude that, since it is an automatic, genetically controlled feeling we should just let the body get on with it and ignore it. When it happens, it tends to take over our entire life, like it or not.

It is also worth noting that the expression commonly used for this malady is "falling" in love. This reflects that our normal states of alertness, responsiveness, intelligence and possibly health are reduced to lower levels. The affliction is accompanied by symptoms such as loss of appetite, loss of interest in anything other than the object of attention, irrational anger towards anyone and everyone else etc. How can we reasonably support all of this? The emotion should be contrasted with the feelings associated with religious, devotional love where the selfish element is replaced by a selfless one, benevolence to all others, refined feelings, clarity of mind, peace of spirit and so on, i.e. a heightening rather than a lowering of sensitivity.

Sex

Reason rarely enters into the process of attraction, which is almost invariably related to one or two aspects, say physical attractiveness and humor – or perhaps these days it is attractiveness and performance in bed. There is no escaping the fact that the instinctual drive for sex, in order to satisfy the evolutionary needs of the genes to replicate themselves, is of primary importance in all of this, regardless of our inclination to emphasize the more romantic aspects. We even exhibit similar traits to birds and animals in respect of dressing up to impress the opposite sex, for example, or jealously guarding our partner from the advances of rivals. We might feel that we are exercising intelligence and choice in all of this but we delude ourselves – it is only the intelligence of Darwinian evolution. Even the ultimate pleasure of the orgasm when we finally consummate our feelings with our chosen soul mate is simply another evolutionary development to ensure that we will want to repeat this activity, which "incidentally" will also continue the species.

Of course both partners would appreciate, if they thought about such things, that each possesses a multitude of other traits, from intelligence and education through to tidiness and the way they squeeze the toothpaste tube. It is certain that many of these will be in conflict with those of their partner and, once the initial novelty of the attractive aspects has diminished, they will begin to notice the other features. And these might not be so appealing! Minor irritations may prove to be cumulative and build until a catastrophic breakdown occurs.

Once the hormonal excesses of the initial stages of passionate love have diminished, what succeeds is a much more stable emotion, based upon shared aims and experience, sufficiently stable indeed that partners still frequently contract to pursue those aims together until the end of their lives. Stability will be more likely if partners are also friends as well as lovers. Those people whom we retain as lifelong friends tend to be those who accept us for whom we are and do not constantly try to change us into someone else; those with whom we can share general interests and outlook on life; those with whom we feel comfortable. Increasingly these days, the spouse is portrayed as someone who wishes to impose his or her own perspective and desired way of life on their partner, leading to increasing friction until the marriage breaks down.

Love also has other meanings that are not specific to another person. Love of a person tends to be selfish or to entail other, less noble sentiments such as jealousy or negative ones such as fear. When love is directed instead towards others in general, simply desiring the happiness of others and feeling good-will towards all men as they say at Christmas, then it can be an entirely unselfish emotion and actions carried out in its name may be moral in an absolute sense. Love thy neighbor is a Christian ethic in this sense rather than the licentious one so often portrayed by soaps on TV these days.

Usually, what passes for love tends to be ego-related, as with most other aspects of life. We need to feel that our existence has some meaning. Recognition by another, being perceived as worthy by someone who freely chooses to spend the rest of his or her life with us, provides that sense of meaning. Being loved and valued makes our lives seem worthwhile. And in passionate love we can lose our sense of ego in just the same way that we can through involvement or dangerous sports. Indeed, illicit sex presumably carries the same benefits that are discussed under the topic of Excitement later (as well as similar hazards)!

Marriage, too, these days is no longer valued for its own sake. Our duty is not now perceived as being to the partner and family but to ourselves. If marriage no longer provides the sense of fulfillment that it once did and we can see no ultimate benefit to ourselves in the long term, then why put up with it? We owe it to ourselves to put an end to it as soon as possible and look for meaning elsewhere, perhaps with another partner. So far, only divorce of one's partner is tolerated by society and not divorce of one's children but, with the continuing insistence on the importance of the individual, who can say how long this will continue? The ego can take us unreservedly to hell, celebrating each step of the way.

Ultimately, love ceases to be an emotion in the usually accepted sense of the word and transcends the physical altogether. The ego in this context loses all meaning. The word "Philosophy" is used in this sense, being "love of wisdom." There can be no higher aim in life than to discover the truth – and that is the sincere sentiment behind this book.

✳ Freedom and choice

The classical view of what is meant by "freedom" for an individual is the ability to make choices in one's own life without being influenced by society. The German philosopher Hegel thought this naïve, recognizing that people's attitudes are constantly being influenced by others so that more often than not what we choose is simply what the influential people of the time want us to choose, which is no freedom at all. Of course they didn't have TV and other advertising media telling us that we could not be happy unless we smoked Hamlet cigars in those days but Hegel was fully aware of the principle. He believed that this effect has been in existence throughout history and that the only way out is for us to take control of these forces ourselves.

Sartre was particularly concerned with the freedom of the individual. We determine and define our own lives through the choices that we make, he said. We can either ignore this responsibility, telling ourselves that we are forced to act as we do by our circumstances, society etc. or we can make a commitment and live life to the full. The choices that I make for myself, he said, are also in part determining the development of humanity as a whole since these choices will always either agree or disagree with the choices of others and bring about harmony or discord. The meaning of our lives and our world are effectively created through our moment to moment choices. That entails responsibility and the realization of this brings the angst to which the philosopher Søren Kierkegaard had referred. There is no one who can tell us what to do and, inevitably, we must encounter failure from time to time. This can lead to despair. It is this danger that has led to   people often associating this philosophy of "Existentialism" with depression and the darker emotions of life.

Sartre also said that we need feedback from others in order to understand ourselves. In moments of embarrassment, for example, it is the fact that our behavior is noticed by others that makes us aware of ourselves objectively. And in such a situation, we are caused to label ourselves in someway. These activities are instrumental in defining ourselves as a separate ego.

Most people would say without hesitation that they value

freedom in their society. If they see that they do not have this in a repressive or totalitarian regime, they are liable to end up fighting for it. We want to feel that we are able to "choose", in whatever sphere this might apply. And most of us, in the west at least, probably believe that we do have this freedom. Later on we will look in detail at the question of free will and see whether this is, in fact, the case...

The idea of freedom is very powerful and it is likely that we would think it crucial to our ability to find happiness or to seek out something to satisfy our sense of purpose. In respect of issues such as these, we do not want to feel restricted in any way. Nevertheless, there are well-documented cases where people, who for example lose their limbs in an accident, subsequently refer to that event as a *positive* influence on their lives. So the situation is clearly not so straightforward as it may first appear.

The point is that one's life can seem without any clear aim or purpose when theoretically all avenues are open but "*I* don't know what to do." But as soon as most of these options are closed, as they are when one becomes unable to walk for example, the mind becomes focused on just one or two achievable goals and suddenly there is positive attention, involvement and feedback. Of course, such major incidents enable the person to put things into perspective. All the previously perceived problems and obstacles are now known to be insignificant by comparison. But the key point is that the ego, with its bewildering choices but perceived limitations, is now forgotten and there is the discovery of freedom and happiness.

Someone who has a clear and positive reason for living can put up with any adversity. Obviously this goal needs to be believed to be attainable, and we need to be able to choose whether or not to pursue it, but it must not be easy. It seems to be necessary that we commit to it as some definite, if distant objective and then give our attention and effort to progressing towards it. If it is too easy or too close, it will not work. It is the choice to give our attention fully, thereby forgetting the ego, cultivating determination, discrimination and similar positive attributes that brings about the effect.

In fact, this provides a possible explanation as to why people may seem to be less happy in modern society. It is not *despite* the proliferation of modern conveniences, more free time and entertainment etc., it is *because* of them. We (apparently) have more choice in those things that provide a sense of purpose and fulfillment – where we live, what sort of employment we follow, whom we meet. Everything is too easy. It is exactly the opposite situation for most of us to that outlined in the preceding paragraph. How do I decide? Too much choice leads to conflict and compromise. I am continually drawn back to a consideration of *me*. What will best suit me? In which am I best experienced, least handicapped, most likely to succeed? And so on.

In the end, many of us try a bit of this, a bit of that; change our job as soon as we encounter some difficulty or boredom; change our spouse as soon as the novelty wears off and the arguments begin. We lack commitment and end up with dissatisfaction and lack of purpose.

As regards the actual mechanics of choosing between several options, it is usually our own happiness that is the deciding factor. But quite how we should assign values to particular outcomes in order to decide which option will benefit us the most is not obvious. The philosopher Jeremy Bentham tried to define the aspects that are involved in attempting to make such a calculation.

We have to take into account such things as the intensity of the pleasure, its duration and whether or not it is likely to carry with it any undesirable side effects. (This latter point, for example, would militate against the use of drugs since, although they may bring short lived ecstasy, there is often a backlash and usually addiction.) As well as lack of negative consequences, some choices may bring clear positive ones, which would thus provide additional incentive. For example, we may decide to pursue a particular hobby that brings satisfaction, say photography. Clearly, if we become very proficient at this, we could actually make money out of it, by taking wedding photographs say, thereby bringing even more satisfaction.

Bentham had three further suggestions of factors that should be taken into account. If in addition to oneself other people are positively affected too, then this should add to the number of points gained by that choice. If one course of action is more likely to result in a positive outcome than another, then the former is favored. Another way of looking at this is that if two possible choices both lead to the same desired outcome, then all other things being equal we should choose the one with the greater probability of success. Finally, if one choice is likely to lead to the desired result more quickly, then it would be preferable to an equally likely route that would take a longer time.

Quite how you weight all these aspects and combine them to give any sort of meaningful result is another matter. It is inevitably going to be very subjective. It is also likely to lead to conflict. Does one, for example, choose to make a few people very happy or many people slightly happy? And who decides how happy someone is? The point is, however, that any decision that takes some account of such considerations is far more likely to be satisfactory than one which is made on the spur of the moment based on whichever concern happens to be uppermost in the mind. Whether or not one should even be thinking along these lines is another matter.

Most of us are in the position of believing ourselves able to make some choices about what we should do with our lives but there are some who are not. Those who are imprisoned, for example, are forced into a rigid routine not of their own choosing. Some have written of experiences in the past, in Nazi concentration camps or in Russia's Gulag, where they were forced to live in situations deprived of the most basic comforts. Often, they would be held in solitary confinement for long periods without any certain knowledge that they would still be alive the next day. Clearly the scenario of needs is dramatically altered for such people and, on the face of it, the development of a sense of purpose or of a routine of fulfilling activities would seem impossible. And yet this is apparently not necessarily so. (See Ref. 31 for the classic descriptions of these.)

It is possible for a determined individual to find meaning in the most impoverished circumstances and to devise imaginative routines to occupy the mind and retain a sense of purpose and sanity. This might be through writing poetry, music or an autobiography in one's mind or by elaborately structured daydreams, perhaps by making ingenious use out whatever limited props might be on hand. It is through finding meaning in such ways that the suffering is lessened.

The key, it seems, is not to have purely self-interest at heart. Those people who are simply concerned for their own safety and welfare and have no interest in principles or in other people, quickly break down in such dire situations. It is the ones who can direct their attention, become involved and forget the ego who survive; those who can use their minds creatively in a dispassionate way, focusing on the needs of the moment and responding appropriately. This is simply not possible if our minds are intent upon personal desires or fears.

But to what extent do we ever have real choice? Just think back to when you were a baby. OK, perhaps you can't actually remember that far back but you know how you yourself and others treat babies. First of all, the only things (physical objects, ideas, entertainment, visitors etc.) that are on offer in the new baby's environment are the things that the parents and siblings like. As a baby, it is virtually impossible for you to be exposed to ideas that are alien to your culture. Just as, if you live in the tropics, you cannot ever know what snow is like, so if your family only ever listens to pop music, you will never have the opportunity to learn about classical music until you move out of that environment.

You can only ever be aware of those things to which you have been exposed and can only therefore choose from amongst those options. The criteria for making choices are also derived from peers, family and education. Do you ever make a choice for no reason at all? Only, I suggest, when you genuinely have no preference. In this case, you might toss a coin because no justification for any particular choice occurs to you – but submitting to such a random outcome is not really choice, is it?

Much more will be said about this under the topic of free will but you can presumably see the drift of the argument. Perhaps all of the decisions in our lives are effectively pre-determined. *We* are not really making any choice at all.

And maybe it is the same when we make judgments about other people and situations in the world. There are billions of people in the world much worse off than we are in terms of material possessions, comfort, security and so on. We cannot comprehend how they can tolerate the conditions under which they live nor conceive how they could, despite them, be happy. But we are condemning these people and societies on the basis of *our* values, which are entirely the result of *our* upbringing. We cannot see the third world from the point of view of the people that live there. Each person's outlook is a product of the society in which he grew up combined with the necessarily limited exposure he may have had to other possible ways of life. We cannot help but see and interpret things from this biased point of view. At the most basic level, we might feel physical revulsion at the idea of eating insects or grubs, yet in those countries where the natives do this, they often regard them as a delicacy. Surveys have shown that those living a relatively impoverished life can claim to be just as happy as the millionaire, often more so.

Perhaps we are always making the wrong decisions in our lives, choosing those options that lead towards results that we expect to bring happiness but do not. Unfortunately, they do not teach the skill of choosing correctly at school. Maybe they assume that everyone has a built-in intelligence to choose correctly for themselves and that no one else can do this for them. But apparently this cannot be so, for they then proceed to tell us how they would choose. Parents, teachers, friends and colleagues are always trying to tell us what is best for us, trusting that we will recognize how successfully they have managed their own lives perhaps...

The fact of the matter is that in this respect we are all equally stupid. It seems that we lack the knowledge and skills to know what ends we ought to be seeking. Instead we seem invariably to be duped into thinking that the particular attraction of the moment is the one which, once attained, will bring complete and lasting happiness. Or else we just do not think about it at all. All of this implies that perhaps our aim in life should be to acquire the knowledge and intelligence that will enable us to make the right choices.

Control

All of us want to feel that we are at least in control of our own lives, though some seem to have an urge to guide or even dominate others as well. Perhaps this used not to be a common aim when people were very religious, believing that their lives were effectively ruled by their God. Maybe even today many still have faith that all of their problems will somehow be miraculously resolved in the end and that they do not need to seek to influence affairs for themselves. But when most of us use a logical and scientific approach to analyze the situations in our lives, it seems natural to want to understand and then control everything around us.

The scientific method has great appeal to the ego. We observe something that we do not fully understand and then investigate and theorize in a way that is consistent with our existing knowledge and experience. We set up tests to see what happens in novel situations and modify our understanding accordingly. We put forward possible explanations for the observed behavior and use these to predict what might happen under conditions that we have not yet witnessed. If the predictions are correct then we have an explanation that is satisfying to our intellect. This differs radically from the so-called explanations of religion, where we are asked to believe in totally illogical events supposedly engineered by a God of whom we can never have any objective knowledge.

One of the key elements to "feeling good", and perhaps being happy, is our believing that we are in control of what is happening. This is the opposite of that feeling of frustration that arises when "nothing seems to go right", when no matter what one is trying to do, events seems to "conspire against us" or "spiral out of control." The very clichés that we use to describe such situations highlight those aspects that give rise to the feelings. When there is positive feedback from our actions and outcomes match desired expectations, we gain the impression, illusory or not, that we are in charge of what is happening to us rather than the other way round. Whilst this situation continues all is well but, when things start to go wrong and expectations are not fulfilled, we experience frustration or panic or some other unwelcome emotion.

The negative aspects of losing control can be seen in many situations. If you have used computers for a long time, you are certain to have encountered a situation in which the machine fails at a critical point and cannot be recovered. It can take considerable restraint not to give the monitor a good shaking to try to knock some sense into it. The increasing frequency of so-called road rage is another example. Normally placid people can turn into monsters simply because someone maneuvers their vehicle in an unexpected manner (probably because they themselves were not paying attention).

Thrill seeking

Involvement is not the only way to forget ourselves. The same principles can be seen in another sphere of activity altogether and in a way that strongly reinforces the ideas outlined earlier. It is in the area that seems to be the opposite of security – the excitement that results from taking risks. A satisfying life perhaps results from a careful balance between the two. Risk brings the feeling of truly being alive; security brings the reassurance that one will stay alive to enjoy another day. It is often the very rich who pursue the most dangerous sports and it is easy to conclude that this is simply because they can afford to. But perhaps there is also an element of their being in a fundamentally secure position to which they can return when they have had enough excitement for the day.

We know that many people seek out novel and sometimes dangerous experiences and sports. And this is much more common today than in the past. The younger generation especially seems more and more to be looking for what they might call kicks or a buzz – i.e. thrill seeking. Some sports such as rock climbing, mountaineering and motor racing have always been popular but now we have white-water rafting and kayaks, bungee jumping, free-fall parachuting and so on. Those for whom the more legitimate adrenaline-creating pastimes are unavailable may turn to crime or drugs.

Why do people literally risk their lives in such pursuits? Psychologists explain it in terms of the sense of being in control that it gives people, taming the elements, cheating death and so on. Evolutionary psychologists claim that risk taking was a necessary part of survival strategy in hunter-gatherer societies. If you were not prepared to enter perilous situations where your life was under threat, you would probably have starved. If you didn't fight for your mate, you would probably lose her and thus never pass on your genes. It is thus arguable that deriving pleasure from danger was a trait that had survival value.

Ordinary life is predictable and safe in today's society (or relatively speaking at least!). Putting yourself into a dangerous situation raises your level of awareness dramatically as all of the evolutionary devices of self-preservation are put on red alert. Having the feedback of being in control of all of this gives a sense of great achievement and worthiness. It is the attraction of sports such as the ones mentioned above that they *are* dangerous. It is only when we are literally in situations where we might lose our lives that we have to forego the ego completely and give all of our attention to the present moment. Normally, part of our minds will be remembering the match we saw on the TV last night and another part will be looking forward to our date this evening and there will always be less than one hundred percent in the here and now. Is it surprising that, on the occasions when there *is* one hundred percent, we suddenly feel alive?

One way of looking at desire is that it means wanting something in the future; not living in and accepting the present moment but spending one's time and life dreaming and wishing. At the moment of fulfillment, this partial existence is cancelled and we are totally here in the present, with past and future forgotten. In moments of danger, we simply cannot afford to spend time thinking about ourselves (the ego) and our wishes. All of our attention is in the present when we have to watch where we next put our foot lest we fall to our death. At moments such as these, we are most nearly ourselves; fully in the present with no ego desiring this or that in order to satisfy some perceived lack. We know, subconsciously at least, that we are already fulfilled. Of course in the moments of danger, we do not think about *this* either – we cannot afford the luxury.

This must be part of the explanation for criminal behavior. Obviously many criminals will feel that they have been forced into their profession by circumstances outside of their control – poverty, lack of education, inability to find a job that is both sufficiently satisfying and adequately remunerative. But, as with dangerous sports, there is the rush of adrenaline provided by the threat of discovery, the feeling of power and control at being inside someone's private dwelling and so on. All of this brings about the forgetting of ego, which in turn allows them to forget their worries and problems, living purely in the moment. It brings the excitement of a dangerous sport or game and, almost as a side-effect, the wherewithal for day to day living.

Spiritual Goals

Many still derive their meaning in life from their concept of an absolute being. If asked what really matters, they might answer along the lines of 'to live in accordance with the will of God", "to strive to know God" or something similar. What exactly do they mean by such statements? If they believe that God wishes them to act in a certain way, from where does this belief arise?

It is possible that the claim will be made that the believer has direct knowledge of God. More likely is that they have simply been brought up by their family in a particular religious tradition. If they have accepted what they were told by parents about this in the same way that they accepted more prosaic knowledge, then questioning this knowledge later in life is more difficult. We naturally tend to believe what our family and trusted friends tell us. We are able to validate most of what they tell us for ourselves, thus reinforcing the tendency to believe them in respect of those aspects not yet validated. Our reasoning may well not extend to recognizing that belief in a supernatural being could never be validated.

Accordingly, it would appear that any particular person's beliefs ultimately derive either from their own direct perceptions or from those of someone they esteem. But what can be the nature of those perceptions, such that they can be accepted as reliable? If someone says that God has spoken to them in a dream, how precisely does this differ from the statement that they have dreamt about God? Someone once described gods as "imaginary super-friends" and, apart from the fact that most believers are mature, is this really any different from the invisible companions of our childhood? However, such skepticism is unlikely to carry any weight with the believer, who usually remains convinced of the authenticity of their knowledge regardless of logical argument to the contrary.

It is understandable why so many people have, in the past, found religious faith to be a help in their lives. Life is inherently so precarious and transient. We are potentially threatened by all around us, from natural events to the premeditated or casual actions of criminals. There is so much that might be a source of fear almost from moment to moment and, towering above all else, is that most feared and unknown event – death. A promise that we are being invisibly guarded by a benign force that will protect us from harm, providing we acknowledge its presence, cannot help but give reassurance to many. The certain knowledge of eternal happiness in an afterlife would be a comfort to everyone.

Sharing religious beliefs with others is another major source of companionship and support, extending the number of people to whom we might turn in need beyond partner, family and immediate friends. Such beliefs remind us that we are not alone; not isolated egos. Ultimately, we have God Himself to provide comfort in times of need. I have suggested that the ego is the source of our problems but realizing this for ourselves is not easy. If we believe in God, we can appreciate our relative insignificance in the light of His omniscience and omnipotence. Here is a true belonging to something infinitely greater; providing unlimited potential for meaning and purpose. Maslow identified that recognition and acceptance by others was a fundamental element of our needs in life in order to feel ourselves worthy. Through a deeply felt religious belief we go one better than this and believe ourselves to have the recognition and acceptance of God.

Viktor Frankl, a psychiatrist who lived through imprisonment in a Nazi concentration camp, believed that the meaning of life is to be discovered in the world, not within oneself. This is an attitude with which many would probably agree. And it can be imagined that, by devoting oneself wholeheartedly to a worldly cause, one would forget oneself and thereby achieve happiness. If all that you are concerned with is how to live a happy and fruitful (in a worldly sense) life, then you cannot do much better than follow this advice. However, if you want truly to understand the nature of yourself and the world, then such a program is doomed to failure. There is also the danger that you will reach the end of your life and suddenly think: yes, I have achieved much and been generally happy... but so what? What was the point of it all? Ultimately, it seems that some sort of spiritual goal is the only sort of goal that could bring true fulfillment.

And now we need to look at those twin aspects that represent the aims of most of us for most of the time – pleasure and happiness. So all encompassing and far-reaching are these that they merit a chapter all of their own.

5. Pleasure, happiness and desire

Pleasure

I have used the word "pleasure" a large number of times already without having attempted to say what I mean by it. After all, do I need to? Surely everyone knows and agrees what the term means? Some dictionary definitions are: "a feeling of happy satisfaction and enjoyment" or "sensual gratification." Certainly there are some sexual connotations to the word. Used as a verb, "to pleasure someone" means "to give sexual enjoyment or satisfaction". (Note, however, that "to be detained at Her Majesty's pleasure" has a somewhat different meaning in the UK! It means to be sent to prison and to stay there for the duration of the reign of the current monarch.)

There is no doubt that we do some things directly for the pleasure that they bring, though we may try to persuade ourselves that they have other, more laudable effects such as exercise (going for a walk in the forest), education (watching a film on the TV) or sustenance (eating a cream cake). Some activities aim to eliminate or minimize pain, now and in the future (going to the dentist). To the extent that pain is the opposite of pleasure, this could be seen as amounting to the same thing, though we are hardly likely to call going to the dentist pleasurable. If we go to work principally in order to earn money so that we will be able to do those other things that give us pleasure, then again this is a means to that end. In fact, if we were to analyze all of our actions in a critical light, we might think that everything we do has pleasure as either a side effect or an ultimate aim.

The Evolutionary psychologists will tell us that it is all

explained by genetics. Clearly it is to the benefit of the animal if it eats regularly to provide energy for maintaining its body in good condition, fighting disease and so on. If the species is to continue, it is necessary that individuals create new members. Accordingly, if a member of the species has genes that bring about the sensation of pleasure when eating or having sex, that member is more likely to survive and pass on those genes to the next generation.

Pleasure is therefore simply a mechanism that has been selected over the ages. There is no choice involved; we are simply at the mercy of our hormones for many of the activities that we supposedly perform in order to derive pleasure. We are driven by these biological imperatives to eat, for example. If the food is of the sort that will satisfy the body's needs, there will be a feedback of taste enjoyment to tell us that we are doing the right thing and should continue. When a child attempts to eat something unwholesome, it is likely that he will find an unpleasant taste to discourage him. This is not because the object has a vested interest in not harming humans. It is that, over thousands of years, natural selection has ensured that the genes responsible for our sense of taste tend to signal their lack of appreciation for those things likely to prove poisonous to the body. (On the other side of the equation, some plants make use of this development in respect of avoiding predation by insects and animals. They have evolved to produce bitter-tasting chemicals to act as a deterrent.)

It is also interesting to note in passing that the evolutionary theory also explains why pleasure doesn't last (and is ultimately replaced by pain if we don't take the hint). If our attention were completely diverted towards say sex, for an indefinite period, we would be unlikely to notice the predator creeping up on us or be in a position to do something about it when we did. A species with such a trait would not therefore be likely to survive into future generations.

Relative degrees of pleasure can explain apparent choice in our actions. Recent experiments conducted by Michael Cabanac with lizards show that their favorite foods can persuade them to come out of a warm part of their enclosure and venture into an inhospitable, cold part rather than put up with eating unappetizing fare. The more pleasure they receive from eating the food, the lower the temperature they will tolerate.

The sociologists might claim that we derive pleasure from those things that we have been conditioned to like by our parents and peers. If your parents always told you that a certain food or behavior was disgusting then you are unlikely to seek this out in later life (unless as a deliberate act in defiance of their instruction). It can come as quite a surprise to find that something tastes good and subsequently discover that it was one of the proscribed foods. We tend to eat only those foods that we have always eaten unless someone recommends something that *they* already know. Our genes and environmental conditions provide the foundations for our mental and emotional makeup so that none of this should be a cause for wonder. What is extraordinary is that we should feel that we have *independently* arrived at our particular inclinations and ambitions or that we are unique in deriving pleasure from the things that we do.

But what exactly is pleasure? Is it an emotion, like anger or fear? It does not seem reliably to be caused by any single trigger. Sometimes it might result, sometimes not – the most delicious cream cake may make us sick. I may not even know what exactly has caused a pleasurable feeling. If I am walking in the countryside with a friend on a warm summer day without any worries or time constraints and there is a beautiful view and... it could be all of these things together, a combination of several or one in particular. Furthermore, I normally want to do something as a result of an emotion – thump someone in the case of anger perhaps or run away in the case of fear. With pleasure, I probably simply want it to carry on, without having the least inclination to do anything at all. Nor is it a sensation, though some sensations are no doubt pleasurable. And, though I might enjoy a particular sensation or a specific emotion, you may not. Nor would it be meaningful to make it our purpose in life to seek out particular sensations or emotions – such a person would be regarded as decidedly weird.

Activities can also be pleasurable in situations where we would be hard put to define a particular sensation or emotion as the trigger. I might derive pleasure from writing but it is difficult to pin this down to a specific action, for example putting together cogent thoughts, finding the right word to express myself, feeling that I am communicating useful knowledge to others and so on. It is unlikely to result from the purely physical act of typing or seeing words appear on the screen; having to correct my typos every few minutes because I am trying to get the words down faster than my skill allows etc.

Whilst there is no doubt that actions do bring pleasure, the pleasure does not seem altogether separable from the action. In fact, Aristotle wondered if the action and the pleasure that accompanied it were the same thing. The pleasure is somehow intrinsic in doing something well, or as well as you are able, or simply in being totally involved in it even if you are not doing it well (as long as this is not a problem). Or perhaps, most naturally, it arises when there is simply nothing else that you want to be doing at that particular moment; you are simply content with whatever it is that is happening.

We all tend to act so as to bring about pleasure in preference to pain simply because, by definition, we like pleasure and dislike pain. But if we are masochistic and like pain, then it is a pleasure for us and there is still no contradiction. (Perhaps pleasure is painful to masochists because it does not give pain??) Of course we also know that, sometimes, people act in ways that appear to be quite independent of their feelings in response to those actions. And, knowing that both are relatively short-lived, it may well seem that the pleasure-pain criterion cannot reasonably be used as an invariable guide as to what we should do or even less as the sole principle for motivation in our lives. We are likely to think someone very shallow indeed if she claims that all she lives for is pleasure, though if we believe she is actually achieving this aim we may also feel just a little envious! George Santayana made the following interesting distinction: *"Pleasure is the aim of impulse. Happiness is the aim of reason"*. Pleasure only becomes an end in itself when there is no perceived purpose to one's life.

In case there is still any doubt, this is the sense in which I am using these terms: *pleasure* is a relatively short-term state, an emotion usually triggered by the senses; *happiness* is much more long-term, a sense of overall well-being. In fact, the term "Subjective Well-being", or SWB for short, is frequently used now in preference to happiness by modern psychologists and they identify three components:

1. a feeling of joy;

2. a general satisfaction with life and overall evaluation that things are going well;

3. the absence of any negative emotion that would detract from either of these.

Those who are truly happy tend to be at peace with life, never unduly perturbed by excesses of either excitement or depression. Synonyms for this would be contentment and satisfaction; not continually striving for something else or some other state and therefore enjoying whatever one has now. *True happiness is the sense of being fulfilled now; not wanting for anything, knowing that everything is already perfect.* This definition is significant and will become much clearer later.

To make the differentiation even clearer, in preparation for what I am about to say later, I want to use the word *pleasure* purely in the sense of an emotion. It is some feeling that I *have* in certain situations. In no sense could I say that I *am* pleasure. Happiness is something quite different. When I am happy, I may also have pleasurable feelings but it also seems quite natural somehow to equate myself with the condition of happiness. Whilst I could easily accept that taking a drug such as Prozac might put me into a pleasurable state, I could never accept that it might make me happy.

The mechanics of pleasure

You will no doubt know that many modern philosophers, evolutionary- and neuro-psychologists, as well as much of the general population, believe that we are nothing more than the sum total of our brain activity. They believe that consciousness is a manifestation of this so it is hardly surprising that they also claim that pleasure is nothing more than this. (You will find that I agree with the latter aspect but totally refute the former one.)

Feelings such as pleasure are simply mechanical. They effectively happen in the brain and we observe them (or feel them if you prefer). Therefore we cannot be them. If we can accept this, then it allows us to detach ourselves to a large degree from the perpetual search for good feelings and the avoidance of bad ones. You may have heard of the experiments conducted with monkeys in the nineteen fifties, where electrodes were wired up to so-called "reward centers" in their brains. (The area common in such experiments has now been identified as the medial forebrain bundle.) The animals would press a key to administer a stimulating pulse of electricity over 100 times per minute. They would carry on doing this for long periods of time, ignoring food and water.

The psychiatrist Robert Heath tried out the effects on humans in New Orleans in the following decade, thinking that perhaps it might offer cures for depression and drug addiction. Patients did behave similarly, pressing the button over and over again, reporting that it made them feel good. Unfortunately, the effects lasted only as long as the stimulation was present and the experiments were not followed up. In the eighties, it was discovered that a neurotransmitter called dopamine was involved and the term "reward center" was replaced by "dopamine system."

It was initially thought that this provided an explanation for pleasure; that it was ultimately just an evolutionary adaptation of the brain. When we do something that is likely to help us survive as a species, such as having sex or eating a cream cake (well eating anyway), a chemical is generated in the brain and we are rewarded by a burst of pleasure. It all seemed logical and, whilst scientists have continued to investigate it, they had no reason to question that particular conclusion.

Recently however, the picture has become more complicated, with other chemicals, called opioids involved in areas scattered all over the brain. It is now thought that the original experiments stimulated feelings of desire rather than pleasure. It is suggested that pleasure, though still an evolutionary development, is used to help us decide between various courses of action. Functional Magnetic Resonance Imaging (FMRI) has been used to detect signals from the orbitofrontal cortex of the brain and the magnitude of these correlates well with the reported extent of pleasure. Michael Cabanac is conducting experiments in Canada, hoping to demonstrate that pleasure is the fundamental factor used in choosing alternative courses of action in all fields. Even when there is no immediate return, we might still be choosing on the basis of long term expectations (though this is hardly amenable to scientific demonstration).

There is debate about which other species have a pleasure system. Some think that even insects may experience pleasure – and pain is really only negative pleasure on this model so bear this in mind next time you squash a fly! But Cabanac also notes that pleasure is a temporary state, signifying a lack. For example, we can only feel the pleasure of a warm room when we come in from the cold. Once we have adjusted we become indifferent. But he goes further than this and claims that happiness *is* this state of indifference!

Pleasures may also entail pain. Marathon runners, for example, almost certainly experience both. We may decide to endure a long period of mild pain in exchange for a short duration of relatively intense pleasure. For example, my wife and I recently contemplated a holiday in Thailand and we had to decide whether a pleasurable two weeks could justify the scrimping and saving for the rest of the year to pay for it. (As it turned out, before we had made up our minds, the available savings had diminished beyond the point at which we could have afforded it anyway so it turned out not to be a problem. C'est la vie!)

Pleasure and pain are two ends of the same scale and the pointer is constantly moving. If you are currently experiencing an extreme of pleasure, the next movement is bound to be towards pain. This aspect can be understood clearly in the context of drugs. These manipulate the emotions artificially in a sledgehammer manner. States of ecstasy can be engendered by use of appropriate drugs. Unfortunately, once these wear off, it is inevitable that there is a corresponding downturn in this state. The only way to regain it is, of course, to take the drug again.

The drug that carries the name of Ecstasy functions by stimulating the neurons to release their entire supply of the neurotransmitter serotonin and also inhibits the mechanism that normally recovers the serotonin after it has fulfilled its function. This means that, once the drug has been taken, several days must elapse to allow replenishing of the neurotransmitter before a further dose will have any effect. This also accounts for the drained feeling that follows its use – there is no serotonin available for performing normal tasks.

(It should be noted in passing that some researchers have equated the feeling of happiness with the levels of such chemicals as serotonin and dopamine in the brain and observed that the levels and rate of their production are regulated genetically. This would imply that our predisposition to happiness is effectively determined by evolution again. This is supported by studies carried out on twins. But note that this does *not* mean that happiness itself has anything to do with evolution.)

Self-administered drugs such as amphetamine, cocaine and opiates also interfere with the natural functioning of the brain, specifically with the rate of transmission and take-up of neuro-transmitters between axon and dendrite in the synapses. But the point is that these are *physical* effects and, once you have accepted that you are not the physical body (of which you will hopefully be persuaded in the next chapter), then it follows that you are also not anything physical that goes on in the brain either. We normally assume that people take drugs for the pleasurable experience they bring, driven by the desire for happiness. But this does not last and, for many of the drugs, the feeling when the effect has worn off is one that is much more negative than before the drug was taken. So the drive to take more is heightened and the dose and frequency must be increased just to deliver the same level of enjoyment. This degeneration is easy to appreciate from the outside. The point is though, that taking drugs in search of happiness is doomed to failure because the happiness that we seek is a permanent state of affairs whereas the pleasure brought by drugs is necessarily a transient and a diminishing effect.

The *value* of pleasure

Some of the things that we do are for their own sake, such as eating another cream cake – the pleasure is obtained immediately following the action. This is termed an "intrinsic" value. There are other activities that we perform because we anticipate that they will bring us pleasure (or avoid pain) sometime in the future. We don't enjoy it in itself and its value is called "instrumental" because it helps to bring about pleasure in one way or another. Going to the dentist is an example of the pain avoidance variety.

Another example might be in respect of the nephew I mentioned earlier. Had he gone to university, as he presumably could, he might have ensured a better job and therefore a happier future life. It would have had instrumental value even though he might not have enjoyed it at the time. If we are lucky, we can end up in jobs that have both values. We can actually enjoy doing them now, irrespective of future benefits, and they might be very remunerative, providing us with the wherewithal to enjoy our retirement. Indeed, if we are using our reason to help us decide what to do with our lives, these various aspects need to be considered in advance. When we finally act, we should be endeavoring to pursue ends that bring both immediate, positive, intrinsic value and which are also instrumental in obtaining further, future, pleasure.

Pleasure, once satisfied, is usually followed by misery and dulling of the mind. With riches and fame, the more we achieve, the more we seem to want so that all of our energy is tied up in the search. Riches frequently lead to others envying you, stealing from you or even killing you. And modern status seekers in the workplace are well aware of the effort involved in seeking promotion; the back-biting and other devious skills that are involved. Over-indulgence in physical pleasures leads to ill health and early death. Apparently the supposed good of these common pursuits entails clear evils.

We could say that it is good to pursue pleasure to the extent that it doesn't cost us too much in terms of preparation, literal financial costs and so on, in advance of the pleasure itself and that there are no unpleasant side-effects or consequences afterwards. Also the intensity or duration of the pleasure has to be taken into account and balanced against the effort needed to obtain it and any potential after-effects.

If we actually define "good" to mean something along these lines, it does then mean that there can be no absolute good, since what causes you little in the way of up-front cost or after-the-event consequences may cost me a lot. Also, the nature of the actual pleasure may be quite different for us. In short, what is good for you, defined in this way, might be bad from my point of view. It is therefore not of much use for a general definition since it really boils down to a matter of personal preference. Remember incidentally that the use of the word "good" in this context is not related to whether something is *morally* good or bad; it is worth using the terms right and wrong for that aspect in order to avoid confusion.

Finally, we normally tend to use the word pleasure for some temporary effect and rarely think of it as an end in itself. It is more normal to refer to the actual rational purpose of our activities as being the achievement of something a little different – happiness. This is the end that we seek as a permanent state of being rather than a mere passing enjoyment. We can be happy doing all sorts of things that do not entail pleasure. Conversely, we can experience pleasure whilst proclaiming that we are not really happy – presumably the drug addict or alcoholic would freely admit this to be the case in moments of rationality.

Thus it seems that, whilst the immediate pleasure response

might be an evolutionary development, the feeling of happiness is not. Pleasure arises simply in response to satisfying a present (biological) need whereas happiness is something not looked for but found unexpectedly as a side effect or consequence of some activity. We feel it as a sense of accomplishment when a job has been performed well, especially if this required personal efforts that taxed our abilities. And the feeling is not related to whether or not the activity itself was enjoyable at the time.

Psychologists claim that the feeling of happiness is a consequence of some sort of growing of our self, an extending of our capability or list of accomplishments; stretching ourselves and meeting the challenge and so on. As will be seen later in the book, none of these ways of looking at who we are and what we actually do hold together other than superficially. If you recall the example of the Pink Floyd singer David Gilmore, it is possible to satisfy one's supreme ambitions and still feel the lack of a sense of purpose to life. One can still feel a sense of futility, no matter what has been achieved.

What usually happens when we are doing something is that we invest our egos in the activity: "*I* am doing this"; "*I* am going to finish this if it's the last thing that I do." At the moment of completion of the task, this relationship is dissolved. The task is finished and I am no longer doing it. I may later claim that *I* did it, of course, but for a brief moment there is no claim and the release of this identification brings about the experience of the natural happiness of this freedom. We will see this element time and again in the sections that follow.

Accordingly, who we really are has nothing to do with pleasure or pain. "What goes up must come down" applies equally to these transient emotions. It is best not to get too attached to them! None of this need cause us much concern; it really is all very much beneath us. How could the ultimate meaning and purpose of our existence revolve around whether or not we are experiencing a pleasurable tickle or a nagging ache? It is there one minute and gone the next; we could hardly found our entire outlook on life on such a basis.

Happiness

For most of us, happiness is claimed to be what we truly wish for in life. All else is thought to be secondary and is usually pursued only to the extent that it will lead to happiness. If we were happy, what else could we want? For this would imply that all of our imagined problems, shortfalls, failings etc. had been overcome or seen to be unimportant.

It is easy to accept Aristotle's belief that happiness is the ultimate good; it is in keeping with our natural inclinations. But believing this is only a starting point. How to go about achieving it is by no means clear. Everyone will have their own view about what conditions might actually bring it about and few would claim to know how to make it last.

Some people – often those who appear to have everything – just never seem to be happy. They are always looking around for the next purchase or source of amusement but never finding any satisfaction. Perhaps this is not very surprising. Such people may well have been made happy with their first few acquisitions but even the novelty of novelty must eventually pall. If every whim of the child has been satisfied by rich, doting relatives, satisfaction of future desires is likely to count for less.

Conversely, if we have nothing, then gaining even a little can mean a great deal. Even in poverty or imprisoned in solitary confinement, it seems possible to discover meaning, stay alert, interested and positive and even claim to be happy. Perhaps in order to maximize our happiness we should live frugally, desiring only a few material possessions that we can realistically obtain on an occasional basis. And if you are offered a holiday in the Bahamas, don't accept lest your normal life subsequently seem poor in comparison! One study actually found that, subsequent to a big lottery win, people seemed unable to appreciate the little things in life from which they had previously derived satisfaction.

As noted earlier, there is evidence that one's *propensity* for happiness is at least partly genetic. Twins raised separately often follow similar patterns in their lives; end up in a similar job; are attracted to similar partners and so on. It is hardly surprising then that they report similar levels of satisfaction with their lives. To the extent that this is so, it should not be surprising that we do not seem to stay happy for long. The continuing evolution of the species requires that we be continually striving for our happiness. It simply would not do for us to sit back and wallow; we need to be forever moving forward.

The feelings of happiness that we may (occasionally) get do not seem to be linked to any particular object, person or achievement. Though some specific thing may bring us happiness at one time, it may not necessarily do so again. Indeed, anticipation of a particular outcome often makes the actual result disappointing. Attempting to repeat a particularly enjoyable experience is almost doomed to failure. It is as though the genuine article occurs when least expected, almost by chance. In fact, the word itself derives

In other words happiness just happens nothing we can actually do about it!

from the Middle English word "hap", which meant luck or good fortune, so that to be happy simply meant to be lucky. So the implication is that there is nothing one can actually do in order to be happy, it just hap-pens (or not).

Nevertheless, we do often feel that our lives are lacking in a very particular way and we may well believe that the obtaining of some object will fill that lack and thereby make us happy. Clearly the happiness could not be associated with the object because one person may actively dislike or fear that which another desperately wants. In fact, there have been many surveys investigating the relationship of objective goals to happiness. A rich man may be miserable, a poor man may be happy; the fittest athlete at the top of his form may feel inadequate and a failure whilst someone paralyzed from the neck down could feel tremendously positive and derive ongoing satisfaction from his successes at using a computer.

There clearly are some links to objective circumstances but they are weak at the most. The overwhelming conclusion is that happiness is subjective. It is our attitude to our circumstances rather than the circumstances themselves that are most important. This applies whether we are talking about our intelligence, appearance, health, the job that we do, the salary that we receive or any other aspect of our lives. So what is going on here? Perhaps if we find out it may provide some insight into why we never seem to achieve lasting happiness and what we actually need to do in order to succeed.

Happiness, for most of us, is that for which we are always looking. If we were genuinely and lastingly happy, we think, we would be able to stop this constant search and simply *be* in that state. We would be able to get on with whatever activities were necessary, in the knowledge that this essential state was safe and impregnable.

happy: derives from middle english word luck or good fourtune.

This brief analysis does not tell us what happiness is at all but it does give us some insight. Whatever it is, our normal experience of it is that it is a temporary state, vulnerable to external events. If we try to pin it down, it will elude us. If we deliberately try to prolong it, we will almost certainly shorten its duration. It pops up unexpectedly, delights us for a short while and then, inevitably, disappears leaving us with a feeling of emptiness.

And it is this feeling that is a key to understanding the nature of happiness. When we are unhappy, we feel empty, lacking something that we believe we need in order to fill this emptiness. When we are truly happy, we have no cares or desires. We feel complete, secure in the knowledge that everything is as it should be. True happiness is the same as lasting fulfillment – being in this state of completion, filled full of what seems to be our natural essence.

It is so natural that we really do not need a hard definition for the word. It is like consciousness in this respect. Difficult though we would all find it to explain exactly what consciousness is, we all know. We have direct experience of it whenever we are not deeply asleep or "unconscious." Similarly, we have all at some time been happy. We have direct experiential knowledge of happiness and do not need to define it in order to discuss it meaningfully.

We can almost certainly agree, then, that we really want is to be everlastingly happy. If this were achieved, meaning and purpose would be largely irrelevant or effectively subsumed. We can argue that in order for us to achieve this permanent happiness, it would have been necessary to fulfill our decided purpose in life. This may be the case but I suggest that it is unnecessary to bother unduly about this. If this decided purpose were truly important, then you could argue that we would not be lastingly happy until it had been achieved. Conversely, however, I could say that, if you have achieved lasting happiness and yet have not attained your purposed objective, then that objective cannot really have been important after all. Thus I suggest that, though meaning and purpose are topics worthy of discussion, what really matters in the end is happiness.

Most philosophers have thought that we actually need to *do* something in order to achieve happiness. This is so too, probably, for most readers. But this is certainly partly to do with the way in which we use words. We do not usually achieve anything without having done some work first. And we are used to feeling happy after having achieved something. Ergo it seems logical that happiness results from action. We also frequently think that we will be happy in the future, when something particular happens. We therefore believe that happiness is contingent upon other factors rather than, for example, some natural state of our being. Ideas such as these are a real obstacle.

Some western philosophers did have useful insights into the situation. The Stoics, for example, recognized that there seemed to be an inverse relationship with desire. The fewer the desires, the happier people tended to be. Through having desires for things that we cannot obtain, we end up being unhappy, so it is important to try to rid ourselves of these desires. They even had a formula, which summarized this very well: (Happiness = Possessions/Desires)

If you have more possessions than wants, the result is greater than one and you can be said to be generally happy. If you have more wants, the result is less than one and you are generally miserable. Even if you do not have very much, say only the roof over your head and good health, you can still be very happy providing there is nothing that you want. On the other hand, a millionaire with a mansion, Rolls Royce, swimming pool and film star wife could be really miserable if he wants to be a multi-millionaire living on an island without any roads, hates swimming and cannot keep up with his wife's affairs.

Desire

The way to understanding happiness lies in examining the feelings that trigger the whole process – desire. We want something or someone desperately. We feel that, if only we had it, our lives would take on real meaning and we would attain that elusive state of happiness. Specifically, without this thing or person we feel an emptiness or lack. Without the desired object we are somehow incomplete and its acquisition will make us complete or, as we more usually think of it, provide a sense of *fulfillment.*

At the moment that the desired object is won, we *do* feel fulfilled. It is only after some time that the effect wears off, as it were, and we realize that it wasn't the final answer after all. (Why are we always surprised?) Since this is the case, why is it that there is even a short-lived fulfillment? What can be happening to make us temporarily happy?

Here I want to put forward a hypothesis with which you may initially feel uneasy, assuming that you do not discard it immediately as ridiculous. At this stage, I do not want to say this is actually how things are. Simply allow it to rest as an idea that needs much more analysis and justification before anyone could seriously accept it. (In fact, I have already sown the seeds for this in several places so that it should not come as too much of a surprise.)

The idea is this: your real self, whatever that might be, is *already* happy and fulfilled; this is its natural state. However, what you think of as yourself, what is often called your ego, believes otherwise. It feels limited, insecure, has fears and desires etc. (Fears are actually only the obverse of desires – desire is wanting something, fear is actively not wanting something.) We desire things because we feel incomplete and desperately want to achieve completeness. We believe that, if the desired object is obtained, we will then become complete. Any desire is then simply a manifestation of the more general and usually subconscious longing for a return to one's true nature.

The feeling of "I want x" is effectively an identification with the desired object. This is an activity in the mind, a functioning of the ego, which obscures our real nature. In the moment that the object is obtained, the desire is satisfied and goes away. The feeling of "I want that" disappears and for a short time, one's real nature is known again (re-cognized). There is temporarily an absence of desire, leaving the natural happiness that was always there.

People often say about such moments that they "forgot themselves." What they really mean is that their ego disappeared for a short time. Their true self was re-established, if not actually remembered, once their ego was no longer obstructing the view. Unfortunately it does not last. We soon start to worry that the feeling will go away or that someone will steal the object or any number of other possibilities. Those worries and fears are new desires that cover over the happiness and cause us to begin the seeking process all over again. The seeking for happiness in external things is necessarily taking you away from your true nature and hence away from lasting happiness. This is the ultimate irony – that even the most desired of all objects is of no value in this respect. It is only by virtue of canceling out the desire for it that happiness results.

A similar thing happens if the desire goes away not because the desired object has been obtained but because something else comes along to distract us. You might be sitting there, dreaming about the 100GHz computer that you cannot afford and the virtual reality games that you would be able to play on it, feeling miserable that you will have to work overtime for another two months before you will be able to afford it. Then, your partner comes into the room, wearing something revealing and suddenly your disappointment is completely forgotten. Clearly, just as happiness is not to be found in the object itself, neither is unhappiness associated with the lack of the desired object. As soon as the attention is redirected and the lack is forgotten, you forget the unhappiness too.

A further point is that who we really are is permanent and unchanging. You know that the feeling of being *you* has remained steady since the first moment that it occurred to you that you were a separate, autonomous being. (In fact you are not, but we'll come back to that later!) Despite the fact that your body has changed substantially and will probably not even be recognizable as the same person, and your mind has expanded even more dramatically (it is now filled with all sorts of rubbish!), you still know that you are essentially the same.

Experiences on the other hand are constantly changing. Now things may be going well; the next minute something not so good might happen. Even though happiness might arise now, in the satisfaction of today's desire, it will soon be covered over by another desire as long as the mind and ego are active.

No matter how significant the desired object might be, the happiness that results when it has been obtained wears off after a time. The wellbeing derived from the most trivial fulfilled desire, such as a cream cake, may wear off very quickly indeed. We might initially want a second one and a third to top up the satisfaction. But if this is repeated, we will soon find that the amount of gratification is not proportional to the number of cakes. The enjoyment tails off very quickly and will rapidly become negative if the procedure is repeated often enough. All experiences are transient. Most are quickly forgotten and the rest, though they may survive in an imagined, idealistic sense in memory, are nevertheless no longer present.

There is a parallel between the "having another cream cake" syndrome and the monkey experiments mentioned earlier. Just as they repeatedly press the key to stimulate the pleasure center in their brains, so we tend to seek to repeat whatever experience has been found in the past to bring us pleasure. Whether this is another cigarette, a snort of cocaine or visiting the shopping mall to buy another top to add to the drawers full of scarcely worn clothes. For a short time afterwards, our desire goes away and we feel fulfilled. But then the effect wears off and we have to begin again.

If the desired object is much more difficult to acquire, say an expensive car, the elation may last somewhat longer but the peak will diminish quickly and attenuate to more of a background smug satisfaction and superiority that will linger until the neighbor gets a later model. But clearly none of these things brings about a permanent change of state from one of indefinite emptiness to one of complete fulfillment.

In respect of more significant changes, such as committing to an intended life-long partner, the initial euphoria becomes a far more mundane contentment. Long-term partners, even when well matched, come to be taken for granted. They are around all of the time and the call of short-term worries and wants pushes the mere tranquility of domestic harmony into the background. Similarly, there is no doubt that an increase in income results in a greater level of reported satisfaction. But, once the standard of living has been suitably adjusted, things soon return to normal – one simply now takes the new income for granted.

Even the effect of dramatic changes, such as winning the lottery, wears off after a while and those who are affected resume their prior level of overall satisfaction with life. And it works just the same with negative changes, such as losing one's job or partner. Though the initial impact can be devastating, adjustment occurs over the following weeks or months and one's general outlook returns to its usual state.

People often claim that it is their job or their marriage that really gets them down. After all, the only real escape from such situations is to leave them completely. And, of course, people do. But surveys show that such major changes in life have only relatively small effects on happiness in the long run. We simply adapt to such changes in our lives and return to our typical baseline state, which is inevitably one of feeling a lack in one or more areas and having the desire to satisfy the perceived need of the moment.

Happiness – the end of desire

Though one particular desire may be satisfied, this never signals the end of desire itself. If you get an experience you wanted and enjoy it, it is very likely that you will want to have that experience again, even if you don't enjoy it quite as much next time. Or you may want a more potent experience. This, of course, is epitomized in the drug user's progression to harder drugs.

Satisfying a desire is not the way to make desire go away. The satisfaction of a desire is like adding fuel to a fire – they are ultimately insatiable. This is why we attach so much value to the future, why we predict and plan and push towards perceived gratification. And this is why we rarely attain happiness. Happiness is in the present and we can never stay there long enough to enjoy it. Wanting to prolong it, we feel that we must continually strive to ensure that the future satisfies those conditions that we believe are required to bring it about.

If we are materially-minded and already have all the usual material possessions, we will find it more difficult to have simple, easily satisfied desires. If all that we want is to finish our day's work outside in the cold, come in and sit by a warm fire, this is likely to be attainable by even the relatively poor. For many of us, real happiness is perceived as being *only* in the future, i.e. never. We are working towards something in the expectation that when we get there we will reap the reward of happiness. This might be the position of Managing Director of the company we work for or it might be retirement with a lavish pension. Inevitably, if we actually reach the desired goal, it proves to be less than we had imagined and we are no nearer the elusive state of happiness than we were to begin with. All that has happened is that we have missed the opportunity fully to experience the life that has passed by in the interim.

The optimal situation is certainly *not* one in which we have practically everything that we could possibly want, for then whatever desires we have left will probably be difficult to gratify. Far better to be merely comfortable with relatively small, easily satisfied wants that can return us frequently to our natural state of happiness. The social psychologist, Roy Baumeister (Ref. 30) has something valid to say in respect of this: *"Everyone may want to get to the top, but if you want to enjoy it, you should take the stairway rather than the elevator."*

The key to understanding is to take a step back and look at the desire that drives us to seek the object or situation that we think will bring us happiness. If you have brought up a child, you know how it will want first one thing and then another. It begins with the initial perceiving of an object and the desire to possess it. This is accompanied by positive expressions to express this need – pointing, asking, wheedling etc. If these do not succeed, they are followed by negative expressions of frustration and anger – crying, shouting, lying on the floor kicking legs in the air, etc.

As soon as the parent gives in and delivers the desired object, there is pleasure, apparent happiness and peace for a while until inevitable boredom sets in and the child looks around for some new distraction. The process is repeated. There are two main points to be noticed. Firstly, as soon as the desired object is obtained, the disturbed state of mind (yours as well as his!) is replaced by a calm and satisfied one. Secondly, when some new desire takes over, the first object is dropped, no longer providing the sought-for state of mind.

This pattern continues throughout our lives. Toy bricks are replaced by train sets; these in turn by roller skates, then by cycles, then computer games. Later, a teenager will start to take an interest in the opposite sex. Then *all* previous interests are forgotten. Even if an earlier desire is not dropped completely, there is a progression, from simple to increasingly sophisticated. There is an analogy with Maslow's hierarchy of human needs here, with basic requirements for food and shelter at the bottom of the ladder and self-actualization at the top of the hierarchy. As noted earlier, I have added an extra step to this, namely the desire to realize one's true nature, understand fully what one is and what the purpose of life might be.

We are continually looking to find satisfaction in objects outside of ourselves. As soon as one is gained and found to fail in this endeavor, we are off in search of the next. We know that this has always happened in the past but seem unable to learn by it. We always delude ourselves that next time the happiness will last. But happiness is not to be found in objects or achievements or people or ideas or feelings or *anything*. It is our true nature, realized when all of the searching outside ceases and *no thing at all* is desired.

So the only real mechanism for ridding ourselves of these desires, which only bring transient satisfaction and cause us no end of problems, is continually to replace them with higher desires. Ultimately, the only desire that remains is the one at the top of Maslow's revised hierarchy. What *really* matters is the desire to discover who we actually are. If you are not yet satisfied with the logic of this argument, you'll have to trust me for the time being! All should be clear by the time you reach the end of the book.

We often think that babies are truly happy. They lie on their backs staring at a mobile, gurgling away without a care in the world. Only when they feel hungry or suffer the discomfort of trapped wind do they suddenly start to express dissatisfaction with life. This, too, could be explained in the same way. Babies' minds are relatively empty, not yet filled with an assortment of fears and desires, memories of past concerns and anxiety over possibilities for the future. They exist simply in the present, soaking up impressions arriving via the senses and taking everything just as it is, without judgment or preference and without wanting anything to be different. They are not aware that things *could* be different.

This absence of mind, freedom from the myriad thoughts that take us out of the present and into imaginary regrets or anticipated future is something that we rarely experience in later life. It suggests another way of asking about our ego. Without thought, can there be said to be an ego? With no inner voice saying "I want…", "I am worried", etc., there is no ego to cover over the real self that is naturally happy. How often do you find yourself without the presence of circling thoughts? Unless you practice meditation, the answer is probably "rarely." It is in the silence of meditation that the greatest peace is to be found in our waking life. Most of us, however, have to look to sleep to provide this peace.

Why is it that we look forward to going to bed (to sleep!) in order to recover from the stress and rush of our waking lives? It cannot just be the physical rest that sleep provides. Most of us will have had the experience of feeling very tired and wanting simply to lie down and go to sleep and then some event occurs that requires us to be active. This might be an emergency or it might be someone asking us out to a party. Suddenly we are wide awake again and playing the new role as though the physical tiredness had never existed.

Also, we know that we can sometimes have a very disturbed night, in which we are constantly turning and dreaming or having nightmares, passing between semi-wakefulness and dream without actually having a significant period of dreamless sleep. It is hardly surprising that we wake up feeling awful and quite exhausted. It is only deep sleep, without dreams, that brings true rest and recuperation. When we have it, we awake feeling refreshed and ready to face another day. What is it that differentiates deep, dreamless sleep from the other states? It is absence of mind and ego. When deeply asleep, there is no I observing and commenting upon it. In fact, although I am consciously present when I lie down up until the moment of falling asleep and again at the point of returning to consciousness, all that I remember of the period in between is the dreams and moments of wakefulness. I never remember anything of any deep sleep because I, the ego, am not present.

And yet clearly that which is *essentially* me must still have been present throughout the entire period of sleep. This is also the case with what we call "unconsciousness." If you have had any sort of operation with general anesthetic or hypnotic drugs, you know that you recall the moment when the needle was inserted and a few seconds thereafter. But then nothing further is known or recalled until the moment when you come round. Yet the essential *you* must have been there throughout the experience.

Ego – the obstacle to happiness

There is something about deep sleep that we find ever so attractive. Indeed we cannot do without it for long. We look forward to it and we feel refreshed after it. And the mind/ego is absent during it. Here is a further example reinforcing the suggestion that it is the ego that is the obstacle to our true happiness.

At this point, you are very likely to wonder if such a statement makes any sense. How can *I* be an obstacle to *my* happiness? If I could somehow get rid of my "I" (if *that* makes any sense), who would be left to be happy? I sympathize with these sentiments but please have patience! All will be explained in Chapter 7. The theory certainly fits well with what was already observed in respect of involvement and excitement – it is in those moments when we forget ourselves that we feel most alive and happy. It is simply a logical extension of that to propose that forgetting ourselves permanently, i.e. eliminating the ego completely, might bring lasting happiness.

One aspect that has not yet been mentioned, which might seem to contradict what I have been saying above, involves what we call "unselfishness", where we seem to put other people's interests above those of our own. I suggest, however, that this is a red herring in our search for meaning and purpose. I am not implying that such attitudes do not exist. Of course they do, especially with regard to one's own family and in particular to one's children. But if such a way of thinking is put into perspective, is it not the case that we are made happy by seeing our children happy? Parents who fail to achieve a particular ambition of their own would often like to see their child achieve the same goal so that they could satisfy the dreams by proxy. Evolutionarily speaking, we are continuing our existence through the genes of our offspring. If they can fulfill the hopes that we once had, we can view it as almost our own achievement. These are powerful ideas and motivators and, if we believe them, it is as if they were true. We identify with them and they drive our actions. They are effective desires. We can desire that someone else achieve an objective; it is still *our* desire and if it is fulfilled (by the other person gaining the desired result), our desire goes away and we are left with our natural happiness.

Happiness is not about ideas in the mind, be they acceptable to society or otherwise. You will never see this at the time, by definition, but happiness is only present when the mind is empty of ideas, i.e. when the mind is not present. What we call the ego is effectively the sum total of those ideas in mind with which we identify. Ego and mind can be used almost interchangeably in these discussions. They are jointly the only obstacle to our natural happiness.

If we simply go through our lives seeking pleasures for their own sake without ever looking for some sense of purpose and meaning, then we might as well not have existed. The hedonist may contradict this: if we spend all of our lives searching for significance and fail to find any (whether or not there actually *is* one), then we have wasted our opportunity to enjoy it while we are able. But the question cannot be taken in isolation. What we ought to do depends upon who we believe ourselves to be and what we think is the nature of the world. Plato believed that this world and its pleasures are transient; that we have eternal souls that belong to another, perfect world. The atheist believes that this body and its experiences in this lifetime are all that there is. Clearly, what we *really* ought to do depends upon what is the truth of the matter.

The discovery of this *truth* is perhaps the ultimate endeavor of humanity and effectively the subject of this book. What is the truth (about the meaning of life, the universe and everything)? An answer to this question would presumably tell us immediately what really matters and thus enable us to plan our own lives. After all, how can we know what to do if we don't know whether a particular action actually makes any difference to anyone or anything in the end? The rest of the book aims to answer all of these questions.

6. Who we are not

We do not usually ask ourselves who we are, though it is the most important question we can ever ask. We might ask it of others – who are *you*? – but then we are usually looking for a fairly superficial answer and would not expect any deep philosophical observations. And yet we are so certain of our own existence; so certain indeed that we do not feel we need to try to express it in words or even to think about it particularly. It has been said that we feel this so strongly that, though we accept that others will eventually die, we almost seem to believe in our own immortality.

So let us try to answer the question. In the first instance, I might justifiably think that I am this body sitting at the computer writing this book or this mind wondering what to say next, endeavoring to explain a problem that has taxed philosophers throughout history and feeling somewhat inept. You will probably assume you are this body sitting, reading this book, beginning to appreciate that things really are not as you have always assumed them to be and wondering what is going to be claimed next.

In fact, it turns out to be one of those problems that cannot actually be solved intellectually, for reasons that will become apparent in Chapter 9. So the best way to approach it is to use the Sherlock Holmes technique. This is the process of elimination. We think of all of the things that we might be and demonstrate to our satisfaction that we cannot be those things. Then, after having eliminated everything else, whatever remains (however improbable) must be the solution.

The sense of limitation

We are always looking outward, whether it is for satisfaction and happiness or for recognizing and avoiding any threats. If we are hungry, we have no choice but to look for something to eat. If our family is in danger, it is our duty (or evolutionary imperative) to try to move them to safety. If there are no present essential needs, it seems that sooner or later we will begin to feel restless and look for something to satisfy this feeling. This might be the excitement of a dangerous sport, working to achieve promotion or acclaim, changing house or partner, all in the mistaken belief that such activities will bring about lasting happiness.

Is there something in common, behind all of these driving forces? Why do we do the variety of things that we do? What exactly is it that we are looking for?

If we are not *obliged* to do something, e.g. in order to survive, we might say that we simply *want* to do it. Thus we might take up a particular hobby or sport in a serious way, for example. Becoming accomplished can then act as a further driver. If we are good at something, we are likely to want to become even better. We move up in the hierarchy of our peers. Initially, we will not be very good ourselves and will probably set our sights quite low. If our interest is football, we may be content simply playing with friends. If it is a musical instrument, we will quite likely feel a great sense of accomplishment when we can play a simple tune without error and have it recognized by a listener. If we discover a genuine apti-tude for the chosen activity however, our ability increases greatly and we quickly move out of our initial circle of peers. It is now necessary to progress, to play football for the company or a local team; to practice more difficult pieces of music or perform at concerts. If the interest endures, we are likely to feel that we should continue to practice and improve in order ultimately to perform to the very best of our ability.

At the opposite end of the scale of aptitude, things that we do not initially like or that we are unable to do well may be seen as a challenge. If we believe we ought to be able to do them, i.e. we are not physically handicapped, there can be a sense of inadequacy and we may feel the urge to overcome the obstacle. The personalities of many people seem to drive them towards more frequent, and more varied, experiences. They worry that they may feel a sense of failure in later life if they have not achieved all that they are capable of achieving. Attempts to persuade them that this is a logical impossibility are unlikely to be successful. If something occurs to them, or is suggested, that is feasible, affordable etc., it is likely to be perceived as a challenge and be taken up. All of the other countless, conceivable options are not relevant at this time and are ignored.

This sense of achievement is effectively a sort of partial fulfill-ment. It as though we go through our lives constantly experiencing an ill-defined lack. Periodically, we have to top-up our experiences with something positive to assuage this sense. Those who are unable to do so are likely to succumb to depression and will, at the very least, experience a significant dissatisfaction with their life. Effectively, we perceive ourselves as being limited. Our drives are aimed at overcoming perceived impediments in order to feel that we have accomplished something, realized our potential etc., i.e. done all that we can to minimize or eliminate these limitations.

But our attempts are doomed to failure because the problem lies much deeper than most of us ever realize. We are always trying to cure the secondary symptoms of the disease, never the primary cause, and while we continue to do so, we will never attain our elusive objective. The reason is that the sense of limitation that we experience is a mistake.

We believe that our material possessions are limited. We *need* a house (or a bigger one), a car, TV, video etc. We think that our bodies are limited and we want to make them more beautiful, fitter and healthier. Our minds are clearly limited; we would like to obtain degrees, learn languages and be knowledgeable on many subjects. But no matter how attractive we might be to others or how intelligent, it is almost certain that we will still be dissatisfied. It seems unarguable that this must be so. It is simply not possible to excel in all areas. A world class ballet dancer is not usually also a round-the-world yachtsman, mountain climber and Olympic athlete. A nuclear scientist is not normally also a botanist, historian and paleontologist. It is rare to encounter world class painters who are also novelists, composers and cinema directors. We cannot realistically do everything, let alone do them well.

Once we have realized that, it may seem that these are the reasons why we must ultimately be disappointed. There is too little time for us to perfect our bodies and minds. Even if we could, we could not do so in all possible ways. Having trained our limbs to be proficient at standing on our toes and rotating very quickly, they will not also be ideally tuned for cross-country running. We cannot simultaneously be digesting all that has been written on a diverse range of subjects – the libraries are too big and our brain capacities are too small.

But all of this is quite irrelevant. What I am claiming is that the initial feeling of lack or limitation is itself a mistake. All that follows afterwards is merely compounding or obscuring the fundamental problem. When we think or speak of ourselves as being limited, we make what is almost invariably an unspoken and even unthought-of assumption about who it is that we actually are. We fail to elaborate when we express ourselves with regard to our various desires. "I wish I could skate" refers primarily to a learnt bodily skill. "I wish I could speak in front of an audience" relates principally to mental skills, good knowledge of the subject being spoken of, wide vocabulary and self-confidence.

Thus, a simplistic view of the above might be that "I wish I could skate" contains the unspoken assumption that I *am* a body; "I wish I could speak in front of others" makes the assumption that I *am* a mind. They are unspoken because they are so in-built and unquestioned. Our upbringing instills these beliefs unconsciously or otherwise and all that we think, say or do from the time that we become autonomous beings reinforces these beliefs. The mere suggestion that this might not be so fills us with incredulity. But the fact of the matter is that we are mistaken in thinking ourselves to be bodies, minds or any of the other limited ways in which we perceive ourselves. We are infinitely more than all of these.

Self-delusion

It is always worthwhile assessing where we stand to begin with before embarking upon some other system of categorization or analysis. What do we currently mean (or think we mean) when we talk about our *selves*? One way of approaching this might be to look at the sorts of expression that are typically used in everyday speech. Initially, we might think it is all quite straightforward – indeed *self-evident*, one might say. But the words we use do not always convey information about the same thing – and sometimes it is not always clear on analysis exactly what we are talking about. Someone practicing *self-defense* is simply protecting his or her body. If they are *self-absorbed*, they are wrapped up in their own thoughts. *Self-expression* is the use of some medium, art, music or whatever, to make some statement to others about one's ideas, attitudes or feelings.

Someone who is *selfish* is only interested in himself. If *selfless*, she will always consider others first. Similarly, some people may be *self-taught* or *self-reliant*. No problem with either of these. Others might indulge in *self-pity* and most of us will put *self-preservation* high on our list of priorities – again quite understandable. We talk about someone being *self-assured*, *self-centered* and *self-important*. These indicate characteristics of a person that are exhibited, usually unintentionally, to others. Similarly, *self-conscious*, *self-contained*, *self-regarding*, *self-restraint*, *self-reproach* and so on are words that we might use to describe the personality of another. But what exactly is such a word saying about the process that is taking place in the persons themselves?

Self-consciousness is a perfect example. Who is being conscious of whom? Is such a phrase a relic of Cartesian mind-body dualism, where some mystical homunculus is sitting somewhere in the brain interpreting the electrical impulses arriving at the synapses from the sense organs? Words such as *self-starter* imply that there is your body-mind complex on the one hand and some controlling real you on the other hand that decides what the former is going to do and sets it in motion. And this is effectively how most of us think. There we are, lying in bed in the morning having just woken up, and we have to make a conscious decision to force this body out of bed. Or perhaps you are one of those people whose *self-discipline* has become so habitual that *you* find *yourself* out of bed and in the bathroom before you actually start thinking for the day! But in this case, exactly who is it who is doing the finding and how does this differ from the one that is found?

There are many colloquialisms that highlight the peculiar nature of this dichotomy. An old pop song, for example, used to claim "*I just don't know what to do with myself*". Someone in a depressed state of mind or in a situation with chronic lack of stimulation might be told "*you need something to take you out of yourself*" or "*don't let yourself go!*" There is no escaping the fact that the way we speak implies that we are not actually the physical manifestation that presents itself to others but something else that has control over it.

Surprisingly, someone who is *self-absorbed* is unlikely to be able to follow the instruction not to let himself go whereas someone exercising *self-denial* probably will be able to (or perhaps they wouldn't have got into the situation of meriting such advice in the first place). But what on earth is going on when someone indulges in *self-criticism*? How can someone have *self-doubt*? Surely we know who we are? How can there be any doubt about this? Is this what *self-delusion* is all about? These phrases are not at all *self-explanatory* and we need to start using some other words in order to try to make some sense out of it all.

People who only think of themselves are also called *egocentric* or *egotistical* and this word "ego" might seem, at first sight, to provide some understanding. A person has a body, something unambiguously physical that we can see and touch. We believe there is a mind that has thoughts and emotions and an intellect that works things out, though we cannot see any of these and science is still hazy about what exactly they might be. The word "ego" has entered the language from psychoanalysis to refer to that part of us that provides our sense of identity. All that it actually means, from the original Latin, is "I", so that it doesn't really explain anything. But it does allow us to refer to these paradoxical conditions without seeming to be speaking nonsense.

But if the word "ego" is only referring to the *sense* of identity, it still begs the question as to what is the *actual* identity that is having this sense? In order to explicate all of this, it is necessary to begin with basics and work up to it slowly!

Not the body

When asked what we are, most of us are likely in the first instance to refer to the body – in general terms. If asked to be more specific, we might hesitate and be reluctant to point to a particular part of the body. We are usually very attached to our bodies. We exercise them to keep them in shape, paint them with cosmetics and scent them with perfumes. We visit the doctor at the first sign of any illness. Millions of pounds are spent on diets and fitness programs, liposuction and Botox.

If someone asks how you are, ignoring the fact that they don't usually want or expect an answer, you are most likely to tell them how your body is. But someone who has cut themselves or even lost a limb or other organ does not usually think of themselves as a different person. We might well say "I have cut *myself*" but this is not literally what we mean. When really pressed on the matter, we actually think "I *have* a body", not "I *am* a body". (But note that this is usually the case only when we do actually think about it –

the rest of the time most of us *do* assume that we are the body). Bodies are nothing more than the food we eat. Beginning as babies, having been nourished in the womb by our mother's food, we grow solely in proportion to the food we eat, building new cells and continually replacing old ones. As Sophia Loren said: *"Everything you see I owe to spaghetti"*.

In fact, we would probably not regard most parts of the body as necessary for defining who we are. People can even lose an entire sense, whether through disease or accident and, though they will undoubtedly admit that their potential for interacting with the world has been severely curtailed, they will almost certainly still maintain that whatever their *"I"* is, it is still the same as it was before.

Where we would probably draw the line as far as this discussion is concerned is with the brain. It is not yet medically feasible for someone to survive the loss of this particular organ, though it is certainly not impossible that a brain transplant might become viable in the not too distant future. If this is ever done, however, most people would probably argue that the person after the brain transplant would be the one from whose body the brain was taken and that the person whose brain had been removed would then be dead. The reason for this is that we usually associate other functions with the brain, namely thinking and feeling. And we are more likely to think that we are a mind than that we are a body.

Not the thinker

If asked where the seat of their *self* or consciousness lies, most people would say that it is in their brain. The *mind* is probably the most popular thing with which we tend to identify. In the seventeenth century, the French philosopher René Descartes established what has become for many of us the paradigm explaining who we are – man separated into two aspects of mind and matter. Matter is extended in space, can be divided and so on. Mind is indivisible, existing separate from the body, in some way outside of space. This theory is now known as Cartesian Dualism. Unfortunately, he was never able to explain how such completely different substances were able to interact. The idea of an immaterial "little me" somehow sitting in the brain (Descartes thought the soul resided in the pineal gland) and interpreting the information transmitted from the eyes and other material senses just did not make sense. How could this interface work? The so-called mind-body problem has intrigued philosophers ever since and no universally accepted model of the nature of the self has yet emerged.

Descartes believed that it is only by virtue of "thinking" that I know I exist, where "thinking" includes imagining, feeling etc. The French priest Nicolas Malebranche said that we could never actually know anything about the essential nature of the self that was doing the thinking – we can know *that* we are but not *what* we are.

One of the originators of the modern view of the mind (and who we are) was the seventeenth-century English philosopher, Thomas Hobbes. He thought that so-called mental events were actually only combinations of matter in motion. The movement of matter in the brain, for example, actually *is* what we call "thoughts." This laid the foundation for the re-emergence of materialism in the eighteenth century, a theory that gained more and more prominence as science tried to explain the functioning of the nervous system and perceptions etc. But it did not explain how the movement of chemicals around the bloodstream and electrical impulses in the brain could somehow appear in consciousness as the color yellow or as the memory of a day by the seaside. A surgeon probing into the brain of a conscious patient would not find the smell of pear drops even though the patient might be sensing it.

Unfortunately, if asked to say exactly what the mind is or where it is, few would even hazard an explanation. Modern science is still no nearer any consensus on this matter. We accept that the brain is responsible for interpreting data received via the nervous system from our senses as *perceptions*. It somehow generates *feelings* and emotions in response to external events and internal thoughts. It processes these data and subsequently issues commands to muscles and these result in action. We say that *we* perceive, think, decide and act – and we believe this to be true. In fact, as we shall see later, *we* do none of these things. But neither is it true to say that the brain is, in any respect, that which is *conscious* of doing them.

Even at a trivial level, it is difficult to see how we could be the mind. For example, opinions and beliefs form a significant part of what goes on the mind. We say "I believe" such and such, i.e. I have opinions and beliefs (and may take extreme measures to uphold them). But if we take part in a reasoned debate with someone holding different views, it is perfectly possible that we will change our mind and come away with quite different opinions. All that is happening is that new ideas are arising in the mind, triggered by words spoken by someone else, and they are interacting with whatever is there already in memory. All of our prior experience, education, what we have read or seen or talked about, come together and resolve into a new set of ideas. Those thoughts that have high weightings for whatever reason will override others that have doubt associated with them. A subconscious summation of everything will result in overall conclusions, all quite automatically without any conscious interference. How could who I really am be any of this?

It is all so obvious on serious reflection. Unfortunately, we seldom do reflect in this way. We allow ourselves to be driven by thoughts and emotions. A thought arises, we are attracted by it and it quickly becomes a desire. We pursue the desire and, if it is thwarted, we become angry or depressed. Our identification with the thought gives the power of consciousness to the thought and that process, in a sense, *is* desire. We are ruled by the mental world. If your son or daughter lives abroad and a report reaches you that they have been killed in an accident, you will naturally suffer severe grief and mental turmoil. You might then discover that the person who reported the death had made a mistake; that it was actually someone else who has died. Immediately you feel profound relief, quite heedless of the other parents who must now feel the full force of the actual death. Furthermore, if your child had really been killed but no one told you for another month or more, you would not have the slightest concern at the time it actually happened. It is the mind that drives the emotions and, if we allow it, everything else in our lives.

It is also true that what is perceived in or by the mind is related to the physical condition of the brain. This can easily be seen through the chemical effect of recreational drugs, which cause any number of hallucinations and delusions that are only realized as such once the effect of the drug has worn off. Similar effects are also well documented in the annals of open-brain surgery or from diseases of, or damage to, the brain itself. Feelings and images that are brought about in this way are rationalized by the intellect according its level of understanding. Obviously if we know that someone has slipped us a dose of LSD, we will be better able to tolerate and explain what we seem to be experiencing (providing that these higher functions of the mind are not also affected). If we are not aware of any external cause, then the interpretations we derive may be more contrived.

Such mechanisms can also explain the reported cases of Near Death Experience (NDE). It is known that drugs such as ketamine can bring about impressions of out-of-body experiences or the "light at the end of a tunnel" dreams reported in NDE. During operations, if the brain is temporarily deprived of oxygen, with various concoctions of anesthetics and hormones swilling about in the bloodstream, it does not seem far-fetched to imagine some similar effect taking place.

There are also delusional conditions caused by brain tumors, dementia and accidental damage. One of these is Cotard's Syndrome, in which the victim may think that he is dead or is missing vital organs or is expanding to fill the universe. Clearly dramatic changes to one's perception of self can be triggered by faults in the brain. This particular fault appears to be caused by atrophy of a particular part of the brain and ECT treatment has been successful in treating some cases. But the brain is part of the covering of what we might think of as our *true* nature. It is only food, just like the rest of the body. So, whilst damage to it can clearly affect our behavior, it cannot in any real sense *be* us.

Not the thoughts

In case you are still unconvinced that you are not the thinker, just ask yourself if you ever choose to have a particular thought? Or does it simply appear in your mind from you know not where? If I ask you to think of a hippopotamus, it is quite likely that an image will spring to mind or some fact that you have come across in the past relating to these animals. If you were a fan of the UK television series "The Fall and Rise of Reginald Perrin", an image of your mother-in-law may come to mind. But whatever thoughts do occur will have been triggered by my suggestion, in combination with your own particular memory set, in a completely mechanical way, entirely without any conscious interference on your part.

I suggest that *all* your thoughts occur in precisely this way. You will see something, read or hear something, consciously or subconsciously, and a thought will miraculously appear in your mind without any effort on your part. Indeed you would not know how to influence these events – you do not even know where your mind and memory are. In the case of the so-called thinking process, the trigger event is simply another thought. One thought begins in the sort of way described above and itself, in association with memory, other people around you, the situation you are in etc., is the cause of the next thought that appears.

An even more dramatic proof that you are not the "thinker" of your thoughts can be gained by a simple experiment. If you voluntarily think your thoughts, then just stop for a few minutes to prove it! Unless you are a very experienced meditator you will almost certainly find this impossible.

Although the mind may not be a physical thing to which you can point, there can be no question but that it is entirely mechanical, whether we like it or not. If you have never thought about it in this way before, it is most probable that you will *not* like it, in which case, as the saying goes, you will have to lump it! So, we must conclude that if *we* are not mechanical, then we cannot be the mind.

We might well argue that many aspects of what we loosely ascribe to the mental arena are not really in that domain at all. Examples might be the enjoyment of art and music or indeed enjoyment of any kind, the love of truth or even love itself. Again, careful observation and application of discrimination (wherever that might take place!) are necessary. As another example, suppose we are talking about the connoisseur's appreciation of fine wine. Surely the actual tasting at least is only a function of the (admittedly educated) palate. This is clearly in the physical realm. But, you will probably argue, the tongue itself is not doing the appreciating – this is taking place somewhere quite different. Here we find ourselves mired in the trap of mind-body duality again.

In order to avoid unnecessary complications of this sort, it is best to consider all thoughts, feelings and perceptions to be essentially the same sort of thing. In the case of thoughts, it has just been argued that they seem to appear, from we know not where, in response to triggers from things, people or other thoughts. Feelings are similar but more tractable. If we drop a hammer on our foot, that a pain should be sensed there seems perfectly logical! Perceptions are usually even more understandable. If there is a car outside our window and we look out of that window, we expect to see the car and usually do – all very reasonable. In fact, as we shall see later, this seemingly obvious scenario does not actually stand up to reasoned analysis either.

If we call all of these things (thoughts, feelings and perceptions) "mentations", we can say that mentations result in a cause and effect manner from a trigger event or another mentation, in a way which has nothing to do with us. We simply observe them, in a way that we are quite unable to describe.

Taking this argument to its logical conclusion, we cannot really claim such things as "I need enjoyment" or "I must avoid pain", "I need to be loved" or "I don't want to be afraid" etc. We cannot even say "I must have a purpose in my life" since purpose is just another concept, which is another name for a thought. We have, and can have, no control over the arising of any of these ideas. They simply happen. And although, colloquially, we say that they happen *to us*, this is not quite true. They happen and we observe them is the more correct way of looking at it. Pain could only happen to *us* if we were the body, for example. Because pain has a peculiar propensity to draw our attention, it is natural for us to identify with the body and believe that we *are* the body when pain is present but that is a serious mistake.

Not the memory

Another element with which some people identify is the memory. Certainly some would say that we are the sum total of all that has happened to us and that the record of this is held within our memory. I know that my wife has remarked how awful it would be to lose one's memory completely, thus effectively "to be no one." It would be as if we had never existed. People who lose their memories sometimes also lose the will to live; as though they believe that they are now no longer a person. Here again is the equating of meaning and purpose with being seen to have had an effect upon the world, whether it is in writing a book or assassinating a president. Certainly we rely on our memories to be able to say, for example, that the child in the photograph is me, though I am now clearly adult. But does it make any difference to who we are now?

How reliable and fixed are our memories in any case? We know that long-term memories seem to reside in the cortex of the brain. Short term ones exist for only a few seconds before beginning the process of consolidation into longer term ones, involving one of the organs within the brain (the hippocampus). A complex protein has been identified as being responsible for the translation process. What has been discovered recently, however, is that our long-term memory is not necessarily very reliable (Ref. 36). Whenever we revisit it for whatever reason, whether mentally to relive an enjoyable experience or in order to recall a specific item of data, the information is reprocessed and stored anew in our long term memory and thus will not be quite the same as the earlier version. It is hardly surprising that witnesses of crimes or accidents have been shown not to be totally reliable. We may actually rewrite the story, with modifications, each time we remember it.

The experimental data for this was, admittedly, derived from rats rather than humans but the mechanism is believed to be the same. Rats were taught to associate being placed in a dark room with receiving an electric shock. Needless to say, after a while it could be observed that they became anxious whenever they were shown the room, irrespective of whether they received a shock. Once this pattern was observed repeatedly, even after a significant lapse of time, it could be concluded that this association was fixed in their long-term memory.

Some of the rats now either had their hippocampus removed or they were treated with a drug that suppressed the action of the protein responsible for laying down long-term memories. When these rats were shown the room, they reacted as before with anxiety, showing that their long-term memory in the cortex of the brain was still registering the association with electric shock.

Some of the other rats were *shown* the room (but not put into it) and *then* had either the hippocampus removed or were treated with the drug. In all cases, when they were subsequently put *into* the room, they showed no anxiety whatsoever. They wandered about quite happily, indicating that the long-term memory association had completely disappeared.

In fact, revisiting old data from electro-convulsive therapy (ECT) back in the sixties showed that this effect had already been seen with humans. If someone was asked to relive their traumatic episodes or fears and then given ECT whilst still conscious, the related memories were found to have disappeared subsequently. Of course, such experiments would no longer be allowed today!

So memories are not videos of events and verbatim tape recordings. This should have been obvious anyway since the cells in which the memory resides are continually being replaced. The protein structures of brain cells are replenished in minutes and those at synapses over a few days. A twenty-year-old event that has not been remembered until now will not be recorded by the same physical stuff in which it was first stored. So, if we consider that we are in some way our memories, it is clear that we are *not* the same people that we used to be! In fact, we are not even completely the same person from minute to minute.

If we use Descartes' model of the mental homunculus looking at the data transmitted from the senses or at memories recalled from storage, the witnessing process is the same. We are observing the perceptions, thoughts, feelings or memories *now*, and drawing whatever conclusions from them, all in the present moment. The sense of a past (or a future) is constructed *now*. Now is all there is. Looking at data from an event when we were young and innocent in the light of all of our knowledge and worldly experience is very likely to shed new light on the matter. We can now understand how we misconstrued events or why we acted in an inappropriate manner. It is important that we should learn as a result and so it is perfectly reasonable that the present reappraisal should be stored, along with the old memory, for potential future reference. It makes evolutionary sense for memory to operate in this way.

In the end, memories are only thoughts – present thoughts of imagined past events (for there is now no proof that any of them actually happened except through the medium of these thoughts). The crucial question for us should be: who exactly is it who is having these thoughts?

Not a person

The identification that most of us feel certain is true is that of being a person or an individual. This is especially so today, when most of us will have spent our whole lives in a society that bombards us with the related values. We believe we have rights as individuals. Everyone has the right to pursue their own interests, dress as they want, get the sort of job that they will find rewarding etc. The irony, of course, is that the same society is interested in having everyone buy the *same* clothes, eat the *same* food and so on. Thus we are constantly subjected to advertising trying to influence us *not* to act in an individualistic manner.

We will all vehemently strive for our believed right to act as we want, providing that this does not interfere too much with the way other people might wish to act. We believe we are each a *person* in our own right, essentially different from all others. We may share interests but we would never wish to relinquish that individuality even if we could. "I am my own person" states the ambiguous cliché.

But what is a person? The word "person" comes from the Latin *per sona* and it originally referred to the mask that was worn by actors in the Graeco-Roman theatres. Since the performances were in the open air, without amplification equipment, these masks were designed to function as a megaphone. I.e. they were devices through (*per*) which the sound (*sona*) was projected. Thus the word "person" was never meant to refer to our true self but only to the mask that we present to others on the stage of life. It is interesting that the word has come to mean the exact opposite of what was originally meant; so that we now commonly think that we really are the masks.

To appear *in person* only means to be physically present, i.e. no more than the body. To be *one's own person*, means to do what one is naturally inclined to do, without being influenced by what anyone else might think. It is from meanings such as the latter that the term "personality" arises and this is certainly commonly thought to be defining aspect of who we actually are. Without our personality, could we still be who we are? Of someone who is in a serious accident that results in brain damage and changes his personality we might say "he is not the same person." People who went through shattering experiences such as trench warfare were often reported as coming back a "changed man."

Are we then simply a mass of opinions, attitudes, beliefs and particular ways of responding emotionally, physically and intellectually to any given situation? If these change radically, we would probably admit that our personality has changed, though we saw earlier that these things are changing in small ways all of the time. Over a long period, in an environment with strong influences, they are certain to change. But surely what we essentially *are* is not changing. I might casually think one way on a particular topic today and quite a different way tomorrow, after listening to a debate on the subject on the radio. But it would never occur to me to think that *I* had changed. If I go on an intensive confidence-building and assertiveness program as part of my promotion to management, I may return with significantly altered behavior with respect to others. My subordinates may say that they don't like the "new" me but I would never think that the essential *I* had changed.

In fact, no event such as these, however radical, could change what I think of as essentially me. Subjected to torture or deprivation, people may become apparently little more than animals but, to themselves, they remain "I." The only event that can apparently destroy this I is death. When someone dies, all that we associate with them apparently disappears: not just body but mind and personality too. *We* are left with thoughts and emotions but they are ours not those of the "I" that has now died.

That we cannot be this particular collection of character traits identifiable as this person might be understood by looking at brain damage yet again. People who have been involved in accidents involving damage to their brain or who have suffered naturally occurring hemorrhages through stroke for example, frequently exhibit irreversible changes to their personality. They may lose their previous inhibitions or suddenly become morose when hitherto outgoing. In extreme examples, relatives may be perfectly well aware that it is the same body in front of them but claim not to recognize them. The victim may no longer recognize his own family, claim to be Napoleon or to have been interfered with by aliens (though even supposedly non-brain damaged people sometimes do this!).

After severe brain damage, with parts of the functions now missing, you would indeed be a different person. Learnt attitudes and behavior might be lost. Ways of interpreting input might be changed or need relearning from scratch. You could well have to recreate yourself as a person and the mask that you ended up with would be certain to be different from the one that you had before. But who would be doing all of this? If you lost a leg, you might have to learn to walk again with an artificial limb. Clearly the overall body afterwards would not be the same as the one before but it would still be you, wouldn't it? Is this actually any different with the personality?

Sociologists and psychologists have a lot of interesting things to say about the person. After all, they do not have to rely to the same degree upon formalized theories as the metaphysicians do. Philosophers attempt to solve the problems of the world by sheer intellectual power. Sociologists and psychologists use observation and questionnaires to interact directly with the objects of their studies. They use the established methods of science to formulate theories and devise experiments to test them out. Consequently they have amassed considerable data over the past few decades and synthesized some useful ideas about what makes people tick.

But note that I am using the words "person" and "people" quite deliberately. The object of their investigations is that aspect of us that we present to the rest of the world. This is what most of these investigators believe that we essentially are. As will become clear soon, we are not in fact this at all and that is where they go wrong. Most of them do not even address those questions which philosophers have been trying to understand. They tend more towards the behaviorism beliefs of people such as B. F. Skinner. His experiments with stimulus-response mechanisms on animals led him to believe that humans too were only a bundle of conditioned reflexes, albeit a complex one. Typical of his attitude is the quotation: *"The real question is not whether machines think but whether men do."*

The consequence of this short-sightedness with respect to our true nature leads many to say and write some things that are incredibly stupid. Typically, they may claim that we are the sum total of our experience, emotions, memories or whatever, whereas all these things are not us but, as it were, subtle objects that we perceive, feel or think. If we *have* an experience, how can we *be* the experience? If we *feel* an emotion, how can we *be* the emotion? If we *recall* and think about a memory, how we can we *be* the memory?

Not the ego

The word *ego* is often simply another synonym for person or individual but I would like to use it in a much more precise way. Freud is as good a starting point for this as any, since he is arguably the principal source for our modern usage of the word. (The word is Latin and its original, simple meaning is "I".)

The classical, Freudian view of the nature of our mental battle to gain control of ourselves is that there are three entities involved. Our genetic makeup limits our potential for unaided action and he called that part of the mind in which innate, instinctive impulses are manifested the "id." The other aspect over which we have no control is the "superego." These are ideas instilled into us by parents and teachers – social standards that also limit us through the feeling of *conscience*.

The idea is that the ego, being who we think we really are, has to overcome the limiting influence of the other two in order to get what it wants. This constant battle is often lost giving rise at best to frustration and dissatisfaction, at worst to mental or physical illness.

We often speak of people being egotistical, meaning that they have a high opinion of themselves, are always putting their views and wishes ahead of others and so on. It is generally used as a term of disapproval, irrespective of whether it actually applies and I suspect that those using it may not always give thought to what it really means. To return to the example I gave in Chapter 1 ("The Pathetique mood"), where I sat listening to Tchaikovsky's 6th while my friends were enjoying themselves, it would never have occurred to me to call myself egotistical, though I might have applied the term to some of them.

It almost seems paradoxical but it is usually those with low self-esteem who are egotistical rather than those who are confident and outgoing. The former are likely constantly to be worrying about what others think of them, how or if they ought to act etc. Such thinking constantly reinforces this sense of little me and the attachment to the ego. The latter, on the other hand, simply and naturally get on with their lives, whether responding appropriately or reacting automatically, simply not thinking about their impression on others. This explains the finding that high self-esteem and the feeling of being in control of one's life are both strong predictors of happiness.

In fact, neither high nor low self-esteem is to be desired since they are indicative of identification with thoughts. If during our early lives we were typically praised and looked up to, then we are very likely to have, and identify with, positive thoughts about ourselves. This is what is meant by high self-esteem. If, on the other hand, parents and peers used to criticize and disparage us, then we will tend to have negative thoughts about ourselves and identify with these. It all becomes quite habitual. But they are all only thoughts and the process of identification with anything is the key to all of our problems.

It is the ego that is involved when we feel embarrassment or if we respond with anger when falsely accused. Such incidents draw attention to our sense of self and expose this if it is insecure. People who don't care what others think of them can remain unaffected in such situations and it is they who tend to be happier – their ego remains in the background.

Note that we can also sometimes be deluded. Some people who appear outwardly to be very confident and extravert may be deeply insecure and unhappy and simply have devised such behavior as a deception to hide this from others or even themselves. Freud called this an "overcompensated inferiority complex." They only present the appearance of high self-esteem and being in control. Underneath this veneer, they are constantly worrying about what others think of them and desperately trying to maintain the illusion of confidence and authority. An unexpected event can puncture this fragile exterior, triggering a breakdown or even suicide.

Certainly it is true that we frequently feel that we want to do something but are somehow prevented from doing so, as in the case of the shy person who really wants to talk to someone to whom he is attracted but is unable to do so. Unfortunately, this whole scenario is misconceived. Who we really are has nothing to do with any of this and it is no wonder that we get ourselves into difficulty from thinking in this way.

Ultimately, the ego is nothing more than a concept with which we identify. It is the sense of I as that supposed entity that chooses, acts and enjoys. It is the most powerful and pervasive of our identifications and consequently the major obstacle to finding out who we really are.

The "I" that we think of as doing things, enjoying things or even thinking things is only this ego. We are rather the "I" that witnesses all of this. We have already noted how it seems to us that who we essentially are has always been the same, despite the fact that our bodies and minds have changed drastically over the years. The doer, enjoyer, perceiver and thinker are constantly changing – we cannot be any of those aspects. That which knows, however, is unchanging. Of course, it then follows that, if it is the ego that is doing etc. and the ego does not really exist, then there is in truth no doer, thinker or enjoyer. This will probably seem a radical and unbelievable idea at the moment. But, recall what is happening when you are deeply asleep: there is no perceiver-feeler-thinker present, yet "you" must essentially still be there. Hopefully, by the end of the book, this will all make sense!

Not a role

Roles are closely associated with ego and personality. If you ask someone in their work environment who they are, the most likely response is that they will tell you a role: "I am the Personnel Director, who are you?"; "I'm a computer programmer." In a social context, you may learn of other facets: "I work in a bank but really, I spend all my spare time painting"; "I spend most of the day at home, looking after the kids but I get out for an occasional game of squash to work out my aggression."

The point here is that each of us plays many roles, as Shakespeare pointed out in the famous speech from *As You Like It*. Baby, schoolboy, student, accountant, husband, manager, father, pensioner, etc. are typical roles that we may have during our lives. Some – whether we are a man or a woman for example – tend to be with us for the whole of our lives while others, such as disco dancer, may last for only a short time. Most roles tend to be context-sensitive. At home, family roles will dominate: we will take on a father or mother role with respect to a son or daughter and a husband or wife role with respect to a spouse. At work those roles are not usually appropriate.

It is amazing how powerful the identification with a particular role can be. With respect to our children, the role of parent can totally swamp any other. Beliefs of how one ought to behave in a given situation can overwhelm any attempt at interference by the cool logic of the intellect. In such moments we believe we *are* a parent and the son or daughter is just that – a child who must obey rather than an equal individual with rights and views to be respected.

Whilst roles remain clear and separate, we switch between them as appropriate and happily identify with whichever prevails, without usually appreciating that this is happening. Occasionally a conflict of roles might trigger discomfort. The classic example is that of the surgeon asked to operate on a member of her own family. The enlightened way to respond would be to drop completely the parent role, recognizing that this might be positively harmful in such circumstances, and assume only the role of surgeon until the operation is over. But most people are unable to behave this way voluntarily.

Not a soul

Many readers (especially those with a Christian upbringing) may be asking: isn't the *soul* what we essentially are and doesn't it survive death? Well, if scientists have difficulty pointing to the mind, we might say that religious scholars have even more difficulty pointing to the soul! What exactly do we mean by this word? My on-line Oxford dictionary states that it is "*a person's moral or emotional nature or sense of identity.*" I would argue that the two former definitions relate to mind and environmental upbringing. Certainly there will be innate tendencies, for example, to protect one's children and teach them key skills etc. But surely these are only inherited evolutionary traits held in common with other animals.

I suggest that what people mean by the word "soul" is nothing more or less than the prevailing sense of "I" that still remains when all of the other things that I am not (body, mind etc.) have been discarded. In fact, it is probably nothing more or less than the religious person's word for ego. Accordingly and for simplicity, I will ignore this overly-emotive term henceforth and merely refer to it as the sense of I.

It is certainly true that we all identify at one time or another with the things that have been discussed above. Even if we do not really feel that we are our bodies, we are very attached to them and talk about them as if we were. Even more closely do we identify with our behavior patterns, our memories and the roles that we happen to play out during our lives. This identification is so intimate that, for most of us, there is no separation at all – we believe that we are this conglomeration that goes to make up the fiction that we call a person. Buddhists maintain that there is no essential self apart from this and philosophers throughout the ages have periodically asserted much the same. The idea, they say, is simply the result of the constant association of a familiar set of ideas and impressions and the tendency to believe that there is someone to whom they belong.

It is, perhaps, only when we encounter abnormal situations that cast doubt upon our previous convictions that we begin to worry whether we have been living an illusion. What, for example, do we think about split-brain patients whose separate halves exhibit different personalities? Are there distinct selves living in each half? After all, they can have arguments and play chess games against each other. But this need not cause such a crisis of understanding. The ego is a fiction resulting from identification with a particular set of ideas. If the brain in which this identification takes place exists as two unconnected halves, why should there not be two egos? What we essentially are would still be neither of them.

We can look at a brain, pickled in formaldehyde, and see that it is a physical substance, complex no doubt but only made of chemicals like every other object. And we can easily wonder how there could ever have been be an individual self or ego inside this thing. It just does not seem meaningful. And this is precisely how it is. What we usually think of as ourselves *is* something inside the brain *but that is not who we really are*. The ego is simply the association of ideas, a collection of personality traits and so on – a constantly changing picture of identified thoughts and images. We are not that. All of this – brain together with concepts, body and the universe in which it moves – are all within *consciousness* and this is the key to the mystery.

Not the chooser

Before we can move on to look at who we *really* are and at the nature of the world in which we are seeking to discover meaning, purpose and happiness, we need to dispel two more myths about ourselves. These are firstly that we have the free will to choose and secondly that we actually *do* something subsequently. Prepare for your credulity to be severely tried by closing the window now (to discourage any temptation to throw the book out of it).

In addition to what has been discussed above about who or what we think we are, perhaps the most common way in which we subconsciously think of ourselves is as a *doer* and an *enjoyer.* We believe that situations are presented to us in life and we weigh up the possibilities – how potential outcomes might impact upon us and our aims. We think about what we *ought* to do and what we *want* to do and make reasoned decisions about what we are *going* to do. All of this may happen very quickly or may take a long time, possibly so long that the opportunity to act passes us by. Eventually however, we may come to a conclusion and then act. As a result of this action, a result will ensue, which may be more or less according to our expectations and wishes and bring with it more or less enjoyment, regret, pain, grim satisfaction etc.

This is how we normally look at the process. I acknowledge that the above description may sound calculating and selfish. I don't apologize for this. This is effectively what seems to happen. As I mentioned earlier, we often act altruistically or, at least, thinking of a desirable outcome for friends or family rather than for ourselves. But this is still our desire – we can only make decisions based upon the thoughts that occur to *us*, *our* genetic and environmental conditioning and so on. Although we may put others first because these are the thoughts that first come to mind, they are still our thoughts and thus inherently selfish. Even if I give up my life for a child, it is because I value the child's life higher than my own and this valuation is either a weighted thought in my mind or a conditioned reaction.

So, do we have choice when we believe we are making a decision or is the course that we take entirely the result of our nature, education, parental influence, peer pressure, media advertising and so on? In the extreme, could we even say that our entire lives are predestined in some way, as if a God had already planned out the whole of creation from the big bang to the death of the universe?

When we act, most of us would admit that we tend to re-act out of habit, rather than make a clear decision in the light of an unbiased observation of what is in front of us and what is needed. This habitual, automatic response cannot involve much in the way of free will. An extreme example might be waking up when someone calls our name or if there is an unusual sound in the house. What about the way in which we rush to defend ourselves in argument if accused of something of which we believe ourselves innocent? And, if someone asks us whether we want tea or coffee, how much reasoned thought takes place before the answer arises?

What happens when a question is asked that does require deliberation? Suppose someone asks you about your views on euthanasia, for example. Do you start from a position of complete detachment? Or do you simply refer to the ideas pre-existing in memory and respond with stale arguments picked up at random from newspapers or from entertaining documentaries on the television? Perhaps you have attended a talk on a subject about which you had previously heard nothing at all. Accordingly, you had no pre-formed opinions upon the subject. Suppose it was a debate and, at the end, you have to vote for or against the motion. How do you decide?

There are only two ways in which a decision can be made. The first, and most usual, is that we refer to memory, to all of the relevant and tangential views accumulated over our lives from all the various sources. Then the computer-mind adds all of these together in some unfathomable manner in order to reach a summation. The second, much rarer method is that we allow the mind to become completely silent and simply look at the new information that is in front of us, without preference, until a conclusion presents itself. If the mind is uncluttered with the usual junk of circling thoughts, it does happen that, in the moment of observation, a new and almost certainly more appropriate response may be realized. You may have to see this for yourself before you will believe it but it really can work like this. Nevertheless, in both of these cases, you have to ask yourself what exactly did you do that could justifiably be called "making a choice?"

Free will implies choice. It means that we can act, even if only in the action of choosing itself, and then we can supposedly act upon that choice. It assumes, therefore, that there is such a thing as cause and effect. Our choice becomes a cause for our effective action. All of this, then, is in contradiction of the idea of fate, which implies that something will happen regardless of our choices and actions; that an effect will occur, regardless of the causes that are in place.

Clearly what has happened to us in the past is bound to exert an influence upon our decisions now. If that were not so, there would not be much point in education or punishment. But we certainly feel that we can still choose to act. We think that we can act in the same way as we have always done or in some novel way that takes account of what we have learned in the past and moves off in a new direction. The sort of metaphor that might be used to explain this is that of steering a boat against the current of a river. You cannot escape the influence of the current (i.e. past learning and habits) but you can navigate intelligently (exercise a degree of free will or choice).

We need to look in more detail at what is going on here in order to try to make sense of the possibilities and understand the mechanism. What exactly happens prior to our actions? Well, all actions are not of the same type. There are some that are unambiguously automatic in nature. If you are walking outside on a windy day and a sudden gust blows dust into your face, your eyelids close with amazing speed in order to protect your eyes. There is no question of there being any decision-making process involved. This is the body protecting itself by instinct or reflex action; an evolutionary development that is unconscious and entails no learning or practice.

Superficially similar might be the situation where you are driving along the road when something or someone suddenly runs out in front of the car. Again the speed of reaction in transferring your foot to the brake precludes any possibility of decision making. However, it is also obvious that someone who had not previously learned how to drive would be unable to act in this way. What happens is that the actions involved in controlling the vehicle become so familiar that they assume the status of reflex action.

But what happens during the learning stage? Initially, you get in the car and probably all that you know is how to turn on the ignition and where the basic controls are. Someone explains to you what each lever and switch is for and how to operate it and then tells you to turn the key, press down the clutch pedal, select first gear and so on. Very gradually, by following instructions and by responding to events in the way that you have learned, you begin to drive the car yourself.

But where are the moments of choice in any of this? Following instructions does not involve choice. You may attempt to argue that there was an initial choice involved in beginning the course of instruction but is this really so? Why did you begin the course? Was it not because there was the desire to learn to drive? Where did this come from? Perhaps there was a thought that you would like to be able to sit in the car with your girlfriend on the top of the hill overlooking San Francisco Bay (as seems to happen in lots of films). Or perhaps it was a more mundane thought such as saving time or money over your current mode of transport for getting to work.

Whatever the case, I guarantee that one or more thoughts led up to your presumed decision to learn how to drive. The consequent choice was a simple summation of all of the related ideas and opinions. These subsequent rationalizations may well have been quite complex, involving considerations of the cost of lessons and car, whether you have a parking space in front of the house and so on. All of these subsequent thoughts were triggered by the initial idea or were already in mind to argue against or support the suggestion. But I simply ask you where those original thoughts came from. Did you choose to have them? Indeed, *how would you go about choosing to have a particular thought?*

Once a thought has arisen, we are in its grip to a greater or lesser extent and, until its power has abated or been annulled by other thoughts, it seems that there is no question of making an unbiased choice. Just think for a moment about obsessive-compulsive disorders or phobias. One of my earliest memories relates to an example of this. I must have only been about three or four years old – it was certainly before I went to school. For some reason I developed a morbid fear of telling a lie. I vaguely recall that I had heard that such a terrible deed was certain to cause one to be sent to hell after death. In order to do all that I could to avoid lying even unintentionally, I devised the practice of preceding all of my pronouncements with the words "I think I thought but I am not sure...." I believed that this should cover all possibilities and prevent any inadvertent breach of truth. I seem to remember driving my parents wild with concern and I don't recall feeling too happy about things myself at the time!

Sometime in my teens, I read a very original Science Fiction book called *The Revolving Boy* by Gertrude Friedburg. It was about a child supposedly born on a spacecraft traveling between planets in zero gravity. Somehow, this novel circumstance had an effect on the development of his brain and gave him an absolute sense of direction so that he actually knew how he was positioned with respect to the stars wherever he might happen to be. An unwanted side effect of this was an irresistible urge that he felt to maintain this orientation intact. Thus, for example, if he descended a spiral staircase, when he eventually reached the bottom, he was obliged to spin around in the opposite direction until he recovered the relative position he had begun with at the top of the stairs.

Now whether I had already had some imagined sense of this previously or not, I discovered that I subsequently had an awareness of this in certain situations. For example, whilst having a bath and getting dressed, I might find that I had turned around to do something and I would frequently have an uncomfortable feeling that I ought to turn back the opposite way rather than continue in the same direction, even though the latter might be the shorter route.

In situations such as this, it is possible to recognize the power that thoughts have to affect us regardless of our wishes. Even though common sense and learned knowledge lead one to know that these are silly, childish notions and one ought not to pay them even the slightest attention, they have an effect. Superstitions are another example of this and many people will, for example, avoid walking underneath a ladder. Probably there are many subconscious instances of similar ideas that we simply incorporate into our habitual routine so that they don't bother us anymore. Most of those that actually reach our awareness are more disruptive. If we feel that we have to wash our hands whenever we have touched anything, in case we have contacted some deadly micro-organism, then the resultant compulsion can severely affect the way we go about our daily business and even the routines of those who have to live or work around us.

Phobias have similarly disruptive effects on our behavior and again arise from thoughts or emotions, in the form of fears, regardless of our better judgment. My own prevailing phobia is of wasps. I trace this back to an experience whilst on holiday in my early childhood. I had seen many other people on the beach eating waffles with jam and cream, which they had purchased from a van on the promenade. I eventually persuaded my parents that some of these would be far preferable to listening to my whining for the next half-hour so they gave me some money and I walked over to the van to buy some.

There was no problem at that stage and I was soon walking back happily with a stack of these sticky items. Before I reached the spot where we were camped however, a number of wasps descended – it seemed like dozens but was probably no more than four or five – and began flying around me trying to obtain a share of the treat. I tried running and dodging but to no avail and ended up dropping them on the sand in order to escape. I was not stung (nor ever have been to date) but was devastated and inconsolable.

For most of my life subsequently, I dreaded the late autumn and situations of sitting around with cakes or lager in gardens or on beaches where the enemy was likely to lurk. In recent years, I have become slightly less apprehensive and can usually remain relatively unperturbed in the presence of a single insect, as long as it doesn't approach too closely. I like to think that I would now be unlikely to crash the car if I discovered one trapped inside!

I guess that most people have something that they are unreasonably a little afraid of, even if it has not actually attained the status of a phobia. If not, they will certainly know someone who has. It is in an extreme example such as this that we can appreciate the power of thought and the lack of freedom to ignore it, unless driven by something even more powerful. In less traumatic situations, the thoughts that trigger events are not so acute and may not be noticed; possibly they are even insidious, but they are there nevertheless. One thought arises, others come in from memory, an internal discussion takes place, possibly at a subconscious level, and a resolution is reached. Then action begins. But at no stage in any of this is there an "I" using something called free will to reach a decision and then act upon it. Sorry!

States such as depression are similarly driven by feelings that we are powerless to control. You may have been fortunate never to have suffered from this severely, in which case you may not have had the added insult of someone telling you to "snap out of it." Emotions such as these dominate reason. The depressed person usually knows intellectually that the condition is illogical and unhelpful and probably not justifiable. But none of this makes the slightest difference. There is simply no choice available; they have to cope with it as best they can, trying to avoid contact with anyone until recovery has begun.

Not the director of "my" life

The lack of free will seems obvious to me from reflection on my own experience of life in general. It is clear that all of the key decisions in my life have been essentially choice-less. It always seems as though decisions were dictated by circumstances that precluded choice. At junior school, everyone of a certain standard was expected to sit for entrance examinations to the local grammar schools. Having subsequently passed the examination and been awarded a scholarship, it would have been stupid not to take the opportunity.

Which subjects to study later was naturally determined by excluding those ones that I either disliked or at which I performed poorly and giving preference to those that I enjoyed. Hence I chose sciences and dropped languages and history. I was good at Chemistry and found it interesting so it was inevitable that I studied it at university. It also seems inevitable that the subsequent cramming of facts and in-depth study of dry, academic material led to my disillusion with the subject and resolve to seek a career elsewhere. At the time, the one area where students were in great demand, regardless of academic discipline, was computing. And so on... All the supposed choices were always narrowed down by circumstance into no choice at all.

I would not, for example, be writing this book now had I not been made redundant several years ago, forcing me to look for other ways of spending my time and trying to earn some money. Of course, you weigh up all of the pros and cons whenever a decision is forced upon you but, having done so, you inevitably choose the most attractive option for you at the time. And whichever course of action seems best depends upon all of the pre-conditioning by parents, education, reading, TV etc. Having thought about this subject for some time, I cannot imagine that anyone could ever convince me that they have any free will in any choice that they make.

You must have wondered why you acted in the way that you did in key circumstances in your past, knowing that if you had acted differently your entire life could have been altered. Just as a simple example, I remember while I was at university, I had seen this gorgeous girl in the kitchen shared by a friend on campus. I had discovered her name and that she was in the Modern Languages school but there was no known common interest and therefore no obvious way that I could get to speak to her. Then, one night I had gone on my own to a performance of T. S. Eliot's *Murder in the Cathedral* at Norwich Cathedral. None of my friends were interested in anything so rarefied! During the interval, I saw this girl, who had apparently also come to the play by herself.

What better opportunity could there have been to speak to her? So what did I do? I skulked away surreptitiously, hoping that she hadn't noticed me! Was I mad or masochistic? Well neither actually, simply chronically shy when it came to meeting girls, having gone to an all-male grammar school. There was another girl I very much fancied, whom I did actually meet occasionally albeit always in the company of other friends. But I was not able really to talk to her, and discover a genuine rapport, until I met her again after leaving university, by which time she was married to one of those other friends...

When ruled by strong conditioning, pre-dispositions or whatever, there is simply no choice but to act in the old habitual ways. How can we suddenly act against our nature? This fact only becomes apparent in situations such as these. Most of the time, what we want to do and what we actually do correspond or the differences are not considered particularly important and the contradictions are not seen.

You do not choose to be born or choose your parents. I know some may dispute this – the philosopher Plato in his book *The Republic* describes his "myth of Er", for example, where exactly this happens – but let them provide evidence! So your genetic heritage is not in your control. Having been born into your particular environment, you cannot help but be conditioned by it – parents, education, religion, friends etc. are the initial source of all of your input. The results of these influences are the thoughts, opinions and beliefs that motivate your so-called free choices onward throughout your life.

It would, in any case, not make any sense if actions were *not* the result of other events, thoughts etc. We do not suddenly do something for no reason whatsoever. If your dear reclusive old granny suddenly and for no apparent reason mortgaged her house and bought an Aston Martin, you would probably conclude that she had become senile rather than that she was exercising her free will. We are motivated by external situations or thoughts and respond to these according to our nature. It would make nonsense of education and the legal system, for example, if people were not influenced in this way. In effect, we act in response to related causes.

Even when we consider the trivial things in life, similar considerations apply. Whether we switch on the television and which channel we choose are dictated by many pre-existing states – how tired we are; how soon after a meal; whether we have any other engagements; whether there is a particular series that we have been watching or a film someone has recommended and so on. There are innumerable factors that might influence a decision. Not all of these may be perceived at the time. For all those that are thought of and relevant, there must be some automatic filtering and priority assigning process in the mind that reaches a logical conclusion and action will be taken as a result of this. You can *call* this "making a choice" if you like, and pretend that this equates to free will, but *you are not in control.*

And it is no use suggesting that, after all this has taken place, you might deliberately decide to do the exact opposite just for the hell of it. It is very likely that, having read this topic and accepted the implications, there will be a desire to contravene it in some way. But this desire is now *itself* part of the equation. Against all of the pre-existing inclinations and biases, there will now be this extra idea saying "let's do something different to prove it wrong." But of course it wouldn't. If you did go against your natural choice it would only mean that your personality dictated that the need to preserve your belief in free will outweighed the desire to do what you wanted. There is no escape from this deterministic outlook.

Not the doer

It is also possible to approach the subject by considering action itself. We really seem to believe it when we say "I did such and such." But a little thought shows that there is a virtually endless chain of events that lead up to any given action, no matter how trivial.

For example, we say such things as "I drove to work this morning." What did this actually entail? It began, presumably, when you opened the car door and got inside. But where did this car come from? Of what is it made and by whom? Many were involved in the design, assembly, distribution, advertising, sale etc. but that is simply the end part of the process. The car itself is made from materials including metals, plastics, rubber, glass etc., each of which has a long history of development from raw material to finished product.

Take the steel, for example, from which the load bearing sections of the body are made. This steel comes from iron, which was mined from iron ore and smelted. The plastics derive from oil, which had to be located, recovered, refined and processed. The techniques for all of this have been discovered, invented, developed and improved, sometimes over thousands of years by generations of scientists and industrialists. Each small part has its own history of "doing" embodied in it and involving very many people.

If you take any activity and look at it in ever greater detail, it is certain that you will realize that you are not doing anything in isolation. You are effectively riding a wave of activity that began at the dawn of man and has been burgeoning ever since. In anything that we do, we rely upon the achievements of those who have gone before to provide the starting point for our supposed actions. Carl Sagan said: *"If you want to bake an apple pie from scratch, you must first create the universe."*

When you speak of driving, all that you actually mean is that you sit behind a wheel, applying pressure to a pedal, flicking the occasional switch, while an intricately controlled process of internal combustion moves the vehicle in the direction of your "choice." Your supposed part in the process involves little more than turning the ignition key, pressing pedals and adjusting the steering wheel from time to time.

So, if we don't really *do* much of what we hitherto thought we did, what is actually left that we can call our own? Perhaps, only the final movement of our body, as in the pressing of the accelerator of the car to cause it to move forward? But hold on a minute. What is actually happening *here*, if we look at it in more detail? When the foot presses on the accelerator, this is brought about by a muscle contraction forcing the ball of the foot downwards. This, in turn, is caused by an impulse in the associated nerve triggering a release of the appropriate chemicals within the muscle to cause the fibers to contract. The electrical impulse itself is caused by neurotransmitters in the brain... And so on. I am getting out of my depth here, reaching beyond the limits of my understanding of the mechanisms involved. And so is science itself.

As we look in ever-increasing detail at any process, more is discovered. The knowledge accrued by science over the past two hundred years has grown exponentially and shows no sign of slowing. What we can agree on here is that the overall process is incredibly complex. Much takes place in the foot and ankle, more in the muscle itself and perhaps we can understand the mechanics of this reasonably well. What takes place in the nerve and at the interfaces is more complex and we begin to struggle. When it comes to the activities in the brain, however, with its billions of cells and synapses, we are hopelessly lost and doomed, it seems, never to understand it completely. All that we can say about pressing the foot on the accelerator is that it happens and that we feel that we initiate it. Clearly all of these intermediate steps must have taken place but we have not the slightest idea how we do them.

It is beginning to seem, then, that our doing is being reduced to our initial decision to act. We are in the car with the engine running; we decide "right, let's go" and, amazingly enough, the foot is on the accelerator and off we go! But wait a minute! What exactly is happening when we *decide* to do something? We might say that it is an intellectual discrimination between several options or the logical conclusion of a series of reasoned arguments. Indeed we might make a variety of similarly waffly statements but what do they actually mean when reduced to essentials? Do we not simply mean that a thought occurred to us to do something? An idea arose in our consciousness and the action followed?

Again I ask you, where do ideas come from? What do we do to initiate an idea? Do we sit down and say: "Right, I am going to have an idea about action"? Well yes, you might say, if you are writing a book in which this is one of the subjects! But even if you do sit down with this intention, what do you *do* to bring those ideas into the open? If you are having difficulty with the whole concept, I will tell you the answer – **there is nothing that you can do**. Basically, ideas come to you – when they are good and ready. Thoughts arise and that is all that you can say.

Of course you can put yourself into a particular situation and make good predictions about what thoughts you will have. For example, if you take a man who has been starved of food for several days and place him in a cake shop, you can make a pretty good guess about the sorts of thoughts that will arise. The point is not that thoughts do not follow logically from one to another but that we are unable to initiate a particular thought of our own volition. As far as thinking is concerned, we are still not *doing* anything. The thoughts are simply coming to us from we know not where and triggering other thoughts and arguments in a manner determined by our particular personality and nature. All of this happens quite automatically and without our conscious consent or will.

You may now be becoming somewhat desperate in your search to discover something for which you can claim responsibility. We might say that, of course, when I decide to do something (whether or not that process involves real doing on my part), I often actually go ahead and do it, there and then. Obviously in such a situation I am genuinely doing something. An example might be going into a room that is dark. I decide (or the decision is made by a process over which I have no control) that some light is needed and that the light switch should be pressed to put the light on. And, behold, there is light! I have done something; I have switched on the light!

Difficult though this may be to accept, there is some doubt even here. This precise sort of situation has been investigated under laboratory conditions by scientist Benjamin Libet (and others who have subsequently corroborated his findings). Although the brain is still little understood, much has been investigated over the past century, for example during open surgery on the brain while the patient is still conscious. Probes have been inserted into different parts and stimulated electrically, while asking the patient what he feels. Conversely, electrical activity from the brain can be measured while the patient is listening to music or recognizing colors and so on. Neuroscientists have observed the behavior of people who have suffered damage in specific locations within the brain and lost the capacity for certain functions. In these ways, scientists have made crude maps showing which parts of the brain are responsible for which senses or processes. Thus, that part responsible for initiating action is known with some certainty, even if the detailed mechanism is not understood.

What Libet found was that there is always a clearly detectable change in electrical potential on the scalp in the area of the brain responsible for action. This occurs between half to one second before any so-called voluntary action. He called this the "Readiness Potential" or RP. The simple experiment that he carried out was to ask the subject to move a finger. One instrument detected the RP and another detected the electrical activity of the finger muscle. The third measure was to ask the subject to state the time indicated by a clock at the point when they decided to move their finger.

On the face of it, the outcome is intuitively obvious. What one would expect to happen is that the subject decides to press a button at time X, then the RP is detected at time $X + t_1$ sec and finally the muscle trigger is detected at time $X + t_1 + t_2$. Obviously we have to *decide* to do something before we actually do it. How can there even be anything to test here? Equally obviously, the very fact that I am describing this experiment means that the results cannot have been straightforward. Well actually, they were straightforward, just the complete opposite of what common sense would tell us. What was found consistently was that the reported decision to move the finger occurred more than half a second *after* the readiness potential had been detected (allowance was, of course, made for any delay in reporting the clock time).

The implications of this are staggering, namely that our supposed free will is an illusion. We never choose to do anything at all. We merely believe that we have freely chosen to do something after it has already happened by some mechanism that excludes our choosing, conscious or otherwise.

The process that has been proposed by a subsequent researcher, Daniel Wegner, is that any action, A, is directly triggered by a subconscious event, X. The event X, however, simultaneously gives rise to another subconscious event, Y. It is Y that is the cause of the conscious thought and decision to act, D. Thus there are two separate sequences of event: $X \rightarrow A$ is the actual subconscious cause-to-action process; $X \rightarrow Y \rightarrow D$ is the subconscious origin of the conscious decision. Because D occurs before A, we imagine that D *causes* A; we thus have the illusion of free will.

This is perfectly reasonable. After all, as the philosopher David Hume pointed out, the very idea of cause and effect only really means that, over many observations, we consistently observe that when the cause occurs, the effect always seems to follow. It is perfectly possible that the next observation of the cause will not be followed by the same effect. Because our actions always follow the awareness of a "deciding" thought, we erroneously think that we have free will.

Lest you begin to despair at this point, let me reassure you that from the practical point of view, nothing has changed. Libet's experiment did not throw into doubt the *feeling* of free-will that we have. It only demonstrated that it does not actually function in the way that we would expect. We will still continue to act as though we have choice because that is how we feel. Indeed, despite the fact that these experiments were conducted in 1985, most people are quite unaware of them and probably most of those who are aware continue with their lives as if they were not. It is part of what we are as human beings that we behave as though we have free-will and believe that we do. It is not difficult to imagine that the process (of believing we have free will etc.) has some survival value and has developed as part of natural selection. Ultimately, of course, it is the ego that believes it has free will and, since we have already seen that the ego is an illusion, it should cause no additional concern to learn that free will is also an illusion.

The implications for morality and responsibility might seem more worrying initially. It would make nonsense of the justice system for example if it were accepted that criminals had no choice but to behave the way they do. "I'm sorry, your honor, but it was predetermined that I murder my wife. There was never any free-will involved." But the fact that criminals *are* punished for their crimes is part of the cause-effect nexus determining their actions. In most cases, the threat of retribution, jail or worse, prevents us even in the most compulsive situations from acting against the law. Nevertheless, such considerations do mean that capital punishment could never be a moral act. It might be expedient for the peace of mind of the majority but, since the perpetrator is, in a very real sense, not ultimately responsible for his actions, it could never be truly justifiable. We are a product of our genetic makeup and upbringing in a completely deterministic manner, even if the mechanisms are so complex that they can never be traced completely. We may not like it but it is very difficult to find convincing arguments against it.

In the end, free will has no meaning in respect of reality and only an illusory meaning as part of the phenomenal world. The Self is always free and, as Ralph Ellison said, *"When I discover who I am, I'll be free"*. Unfortunately, as someone else said, *"Before you can break out of prison, you must first realize you are locked up"*. The person is not free. Fortunately, the person does not exist. Even at an everyday level, if you believe that you do not have free-will, this is actually quite freeing. You no longer have to worry about making decisions – you just do it. You don't need to think about responsibility. Your nature has been partly determined by the standards inculcated in you by parent and teachers; your actions cannot help but be responsible according to those standards. If we should act in contravention of those standards, we can probably bank upon the conditioned response of guilt to bring us back into line!

If you have accepted the arguments that have been presented earlier about are not being the body, mind, ego etc., none of this should really cause any problem - it has to be the case that we have no free will. Since it has been shown that the ego is illusory, who would there be to make any decision?

In many ways, fully appreciating the essence of this topic is the key to understanding our Self. Whilst we genuinely believe that we have free will, we continue to see ourselves as independent agents i.e. as separate and as doers and enjoyers. We are none of these things and an intellectual appreciation of that is a valuable first step towards liberation. Doing still takes place, as does enjoying. It is simply that there is no doer or enjoyer – this is all in the domain of that illusory and false ego.

Not the perceiver, feeler or enjoyer

Here are a few other firmly established ideas. We do not usually think of ourselves in quite these ways but, if someone asked whether it was really "you" who was seeing the wheelbarrow outside your window, really "you" who was feeling the pain in "your" tooth or really "you" who was enjoying the cream cake, you would probably think that they were mad.

Of course no one is absolutely certain in objective terms about any aspect involving mental aspects of events in the brain, but the mechanism suggested by Wegner to explain the illusion of decision making could provide similar explanations for all of these other phenomena.

Take perception for example. We have already discussed reflex reactions and learned responses that have become automatic. In such cases, our brains perceive something and the body reacts. "We" might not even be paying attention. Could we truly say that we were present as the perceiver?

Lest you think that this is becoming too incredulous, I refer you to a little-known, but well investigated phenomenon that suggests it is actually quite reasonable. It is called "blind sight." It occurs in instances where part of the primary visual cortex of the brain (called the striate cortex) has been damaged but the eyes themselves still function normally. Visual input to the eyes is mapped initially onto this area of the brain and the map is effectively what we "see." Since mapping does not take place in the damaged area, we do not see that part of the image. People who have suffered damage to this part of the brain thus report that they are blind.

The phenomenon originally came to light when it was discovered that monkeys who had suffered damage to this part of the brain appeared still to be able to detect some visual input. Experiments were subsequently carried out on humans with similar damage who had been assumed to be blind and who reported being so. These experiments took the form of, for example, projecting vertical or horizontal grids and asking the subjects to "guess" which was being shown. Although they claimed only to be guessing, results proved that this could not be the case. They could somehow sense motion and differentiate between light and dark. Though adamant that they could not see (they were not the perceiver), it was evident that some subconscious process was still able to take place.

Some such mechanism as Wegner's might be operating here. We could say that "real" perception, P, is directly triggered subconsciously by the reception of the initial stimulus in the cortex, X. The event X, however, might simultaneously give rise to another subconscious event, Y. And it could be Y that is the cause of the conscious awareness, A, of the perception. Thus there are two separate sequences in perception: $X \rightarrow P$ is the actual subconscious object-to-perception process; $X \rightarrow Y \rightarrow A$ is the subconscious origin of the conscious awareness. Both processes are clearly affected in the case of blind sight. The second seems to be completely disrupted – we claim not to be able to see at all. But the first is obviously only partly disrupted – there is the remnant of a subconscious ability to see something.

We know that there are times when we do things on "auto pilot." We can drive from A to B perfectly safely but have no recollection of doing so. Clearly something was seeing the road, the traffic and the turnings and instructing the body to operate the relevant controls. We can call this the perceiver – but I was not it at the time. Why then should I be it at any other time?

Similar arguments can be provided for other aspects of who we think we are. Creative thinking is an obvious one. We have already discussed above how we are not the thinker but even less can we choose to think creatively, discover original solutions to problems and invent new methods or theories. Typically we here of ideas "coming to people" after they have switched off any active trying or thinking. Archimedes jumps out of his bath or Kekulé sees an image in the embers of the fire. It is as if the creative process goes on entirely at a subconscious level and, only when the solution is finally reached, does the answer suddenly appear to our conscious awareness.

When a thought arises, its novelty or attractiveness can appeal strongly for our attention. If we are not too busy, we may acquiesce and spend some time daydreaming in response. But if we are in the middle of some activity that requires concentration, it is usually not too difficult to put the thought on hold, as it were, and continue with the job in hand. Feeling is more visceral. There is usually much less detachment. But it is usually still possible to carry on with a task, whilst still being aware of some underlying feeling. We might, for example be feeling depressed or in the throes of unrequited love. But, depending upon the importance of the activity, we stoically put aside our feelings and give our attention to the task. Ultimately we are not the feeler either, unless we voluntarily give our attention to the feeling.

The case of enjoyment is perhaps the most difficult, since enjoying is usually the purpose of the related action. If we indulge in an activity for the purpose of deriving enjoyment, and we do, then it is all too natural for us to identify with that enjoyment for as long as it lasts and to think that *we* are the enjoyer. And this experience and the use of the word mean that it is not analogous to the preceding examples. It would not make sense for us to claim that we were enjoying something but were not consciously aware of doing so. In order to recognize the identification, it requires a degree of detachment that we do not usually cultivate in those circumstances. Alternatively, identification with some other activity or role, deemed to be more important, can reveal the truth of the matter.

You will no doubt recognize the situation of not enjoying, to quite the same degree as usual, something that you usually enjoy because your mind is "elsewhere." If you are worrying about or otherwise anticipating some future event, for example, then you will be unable to lose yourself in the enjoyment. This has all been discussed above under the topic of involvement. True enjoyment, also known as happiness, comes about when we "forget ourselves", when the illusory ego disappears and we are simply ourselves. The "enjoyer" is another guise of the ego, claiming that "I enjoyed that" after the event. Notice that there is no enjoyment at the time that this claim is made. During the enjoyment, there was simply happiness, our natural state in the absence of the covering up of this by the ignorance of the ego.

True most of the time when we had a really good time we were not expecting to have a good time,

7. Who we are

It is much easier to say what we are not than to understand who we really are. All that we have to do is look. If we can see something, be it physical like the body, subtle such as a thought or concept, or abstract like a role or the ego, we know that we cannot be it. But how do we see that which is seeing? In fact, as we shall discover later, we can't. Nevertheless, the intellect can take us a long way. When we have eliminated all of those things that we are aware of, what we are left with is that which is aware, that without which the body and mind would be inert. This is consciousness. Consciousness must be what we truly are.

Consciousness

We tend to equate consciousness with the experience of perception, having a pain or other sensation, being aware of a thought and so on. Because these activities are all associated with the brain, we mix them up and think that consciousness = having perceptions etc. = activity of the brain.

We also tend to confuse consciousness with "being conscious" so that, when we are deeply asleep or under anesthetic, we say that we are unconscious. But even when we are deeply asleep, there remains something that is essentially us. This immediately re-identifies itself with body and mind upon waking so that we still feel ourselves to be the same "person" that went to sleep.

Historically, it is understandable why scientists would associate consciousness with the brain, as was discussed earlier in respect of surgery. What we are conscious *of* is certainly dependent upon which part of the brain is being stimulated. We also have to use the brain in order to communicate with others the fact that we are conscious. When the brain dies, even though the body may be intact, consciousness ceases to operate through it and we conclude that the related person is now dead.

This way of describing it, which might seem a little strange, is quite deliberate. The normal way of interpreting the perceived phenomena, and the paradigm into which scientists are locked, is that the brain somehow generates consciousness once a particular level of complexity has been reached. With that model it follows that, when the brain is damaged, consciousness is affected and when the brain is destroyed, consciousness ceases to exist. But it can be seen that this alternative explanation is equally sound. When the brain is damaged, consciousness is no longer able to utilize it to perform all of those functions that were previously possible. When the brain is destroyed, consciousness can no longer function in the body-mind at all.

There are, however, quite crucial differences in the consequences. On the traditional model, once the brain is dead, consciousness ceases too – permanently. According to the model I am now suggesting, consciousness is actually never affected by the brain at all. It is merely the manifestations that change. When the brain dies, consciousness can no longer utilize it so that there are no more manifestations in that body but consciousness still continues to function elsewhere, as we are perfectly well aware. Other body-minds continue to go about their business as before.

We have already seen in the last chapter that we cannot be the body or the mind. By a process of elimination, we have deduced that we must be consciousness. Consequently, what we essentially are is not dependent upon the body or mind except for those functions that are performed by them – perception, thought, communication etc. You might be tempted to ask what would be left if all of these things were taken away. You do not need to look very far for an answer. You experience your true nature of consciousness every night in deep sleep – you are just not aware of the fact!

Thus it is not strictly correct to say that it is the brain that makes us conscious. Most of us are used to thinking that what we essentially are is the brain, which has the property of consciousness but this is to see the phenomenon incorrectly. It is like saying that light is essentially the light bulb, which has this peculiar property of electricity. In fact, it is electricity, functioning through the light bulb, which brings about the manifestation of light. Similarly it is consciousness, functioning through the brain, which causes the manifestation of all of those things that we associate with a living being. Just as the light bulb is dead, inert and useless without the electricity, so the body and brain are dead and inert food without the consciousness. (And, just as the light bulb cannot conceive of or understand the nature of electricity, neither can the mind conceive of or understand the nature of consciousness.)

Furthermore, when we look at so-called objects, what we actually *see* is always and only the light that ultimately enters our eyes. We never see any "object" as such and without the light itself we would see nothing at all. And yet, paradoxically, without the objects, we would see nothing either. If we were in deep space, looking away from a sun into the depths of space and if there were no objects at all, we would see nothing but blackness. There would be nothing to reflect the light back to our eyes.

Similarly, when we are deeply asleep, we are "unconscious." There is nothing currently "reflecting" back the "light", i.e. we are not aware of consciousness. In waking or dreaming sleep, however, where there are perceptions, thoughts and feelings, we realize that we are conscious by virtue of being aware of the object.

It is consciousness that we essentially are, not the meat in which it operates. (Note that the whole of this section is an interim description only. When we look at the nature of reality itself in chapter 9, we will see that consciousness is even more funda- mental.) All of the scientists' talk about consciousness evolving as life became more complex is completely missing the point. Consciousness has always been here. What has happened is that, as life has evolved, consciousness has manifested in more and more complex ways.

We assume that there is no consciousness in plants and stones because they do not manifest behavior that our minds would associate with consciousness. But this is simply because they lack the complexity. In the case of people with severe brain damage, which renders them incapable of expressing the behavior that we normally associate with fully conscious people, this does not mean that their consciousness has been destroyed or, indeed, affected in any way. It is merely the capability for manifestation that has been affected. A comatose person can seem plant like and yet recover completely. Even in the extremity of death of the organism, consciousness itself remains unchanged. The breakdown of the tissues could not take place without it.

As a very crude metaphor, if you step on a torch and break it, you will no longer be able to use it to find your way through a dark passage. But you can still use the battery to power your radio.

Ultimately, it is never going to be possible to explain consciousness, since this is what we essentially are. The tool that we have for investigating and understanding things is the mind, but I am not that. I can see the mind working, thoughts arising and decisions apparently being made. Therefore I am beyond this and cannot in any sense *be* the mind. I am the witness of the mind. As soon as I begin to speak about explaining consciousness, I am in a state of identification with the mind and using its tools.

All of the many, wonderful theories that attempt to explain how consciousness originates from the material brain fail, for the simple reason that they are asking the question the wrong way round. Not that they would necessarily come much closer to an answer but the correct question ought to be "how does the brain arise within consciousness?"

Having consciousness is not the same as having a mind or senses, or of being self-aware. Consciousness does not emerge from the brain. Nor does it depend upon any properties of matter not yet discovered by science. We will see later that matter does not exist independently of consciousness. Nor is it true to say that we "have" consciousness. Ultimately, both matter and ourselves will be realized to be nothing other than consciousness itself.

Attachment to things we are not

OK, so we are really *consciousness* in some, as yet unexplained way and not any of the things we might previously have thought ourselves to be. Why is it, then, that everyone tends to think that they are bodies, minds and so on? The explanation is that, in all of these cases, consciousness is being identified with something else and then the mistake is made of thinking that I *am* the thing with which I have identified.

A piece of wood is not attracted by a magnet, whereas a piece of iron is. However, if you attach the wood to the iron with an elastic band and the magnet is strong enough, you can hold the magnet next to the wood, now with its attachment of iron, and it will be attracted. Even so, the wood is not magnetic and really is not itself affected by the magnet at all. It is only by virtue of its being attached to the iron that it appears to be attracted.

So it is with us. Who-we-really-are is unaffected by any of the apparent things in the world. But because we have identified ourselves with our body, mind, emotions and so on and because those aspects *are* affected by worldly things, so it seems that *I* am affected. For example, I might tell you that you only *believe* that you die. In fact, it is really only the body that dies. Of course, I don't expect you to accept that (yet). But, in saying "I do not accept that statement", what is now happening is that you are identifying with the mind, which is making judgments about the ideas and thoughts triggered by the earlier sentence.

We use the word "I" without thinking what we actually mean by it. Certainly we all treat ourselves as separate, autonomous creatures and feel that we really do know who we are. But, in practically all of the situations in which we have cause to think about it at all, what is actually taking place is this process of identification and not a consideration of our true nature. This provides us with a much better "definition of the ego:" "I and mine" as opposed to "you and yours." The ego *is* this process of identification and not something separate at all. In fact, if analyzed fully, it comes to be appreciated that this ego is an illusion and has no real existence. Of course there is thinking and perceiving and feeling and experiencing but the "I" that we believe to be the subject of all of these things is a mental construct resulting from identification.

"I" want and expect to get all sorts of things, including explanations as to who *I* am and what the purpose of *my* life should be. It is the ultimate irony that it is this very non-entity that prevents our happiness. It is during the moments that we forget ourselves (i.e. when there is no process of identification taking place and therefore the ego doesn't exist) that we feel most alive and fulfilled. When we are engrossed in an activity, for example watching a film or raving at a party, we forget ourselves and claim to be enjoying life. And when we are edging our way along a ledge hundreds of feet up a cliff, yet feeling in control and doing this because we want to rather than because we have been forced into it, we also forget the ego and feel tremendous positive feedback. Without the ego, when we are living totally in the moment, there is no attachment to limiting thoughts or feelings.

I came across a beautiful little illustration of this principle in a post to an Internet Egroup, quoting the Zen philosopher David Loy: *A Native American grandfather was talking to his grandson about how he felt about the tragedy on September 11th. He said, "I feel as if I have two wolves fighting in my heart. One wolf is vengeful, angry, violent. The other wolf is loving, forgiving, compassionate." The grandson asked him, "Which wolf will win the fight in your heart?" The grandfather answered, "the one I feed."* Whatever aspect of our body-mind receives our attention will grow in significance until it becomes a factor influencing our entire outlook on life. If it is the body we can become a health freak or a slave to fashion; if it is an idea, we can become a terrorist prepared to blow ourselves and others into oblivion.

Levels of "being"

A very ancient model from an Indian philosophy regards our essential nature as being covered over by a series of sheaths in the same way that the sheath of a dagger covers the blade. As we move from the outer to the inner, we proceed from the gross material aspects through ever more subtle ones until we reach the real content inside all of these envelopes. This progression can also be regarded as a model for the increasing complexity of life as we know it on the Earth.

The first level is that of insensible matter. This is the level of the earth itself – soil, sand or rocks etc. and of tables, televisions and tractors. Like it or not, this is also the level of the matter of our bodies. On their own, i.e. after our so-called death, they are inert.

The second level is life – that property that differentiates inanimate, insentient objects such as bricks from those that are able to respond to their environment and change accordingly. After single-celled organisms and amoeba, the most basic life forms are plants. These grow in the presence of light, water and nutrients and return to the first level of matter if these factors are permanently removed. All animals also exhibit the properties of this level. As long as the animating force, whatever this may be, is present the matter that manifests it is said to be alive. Once the manifestation ceases, it is said to have died.

Science has described much of this process and we can learn about the reproductive behavior of cells, the function of proteins in food breakdown and of hormones in the triggering of bodily processes etc. This investigation may continue to increasingly detailed levels so that we can now look at sequences of nucleotides on a strand of a person's DNA and make predictions about his susceptibility to diseases or tendency to form stable relationships. And yet there is no indication that some ultimate life force will ever be identified that can in any way be pinned down or transplanted.

Exactly what it is that constitutes this elusive property is likely to be insoluble. Indeed, perhaps it is not really meaningful to attempt to solve it. Maybe it is only a linguistic term to describe processes of a certain degree of complexity that exhibit specific phenomena. After all, a crystal of salt placed in a solution of salt water will grow and, if we pour boiling water onto it, we could choose to say that it dies. We are hardly likely to consider the crystal to be alive in the usual sense of the word but is this process essentially different from growing bacteria in a Petri dish? In terms of complexity, clearly it is different but is there any *essential* difference?

Alan Watts, a popular guru/philosopher of the nineteen seventies, suggested that eating was simply the process by which the pattern of the food is converted into the pattern of the eater. As was noted above, the body literally is the food we have eaten. Life could simply be defined as the word we use to state that this process is actively taking place for the related organism. Death occurs once this pattern-changing process ceases. Watts actually uses this description to question the concept of cause and effect, which we looked at earlier. We might be tempted to say that lack of food *causes* death but, suggests Watts, this is misleading and effectively meaningless. All that happens is that a new process supersedes the old one and the body of the eater now changes its pattern and becomes food for worms or fungi.

Such a way of looking at things is clearly alien and we may have difficulty relating to it. Think for a moment, though: at what precise point in your existence would you say that your life actually began? Note that this is not quite the same thing as asking about your earliest memory – few of us remember our very early childhood. All of us would claim that we were alive at the moment of birth and most would concede that we were alive in the womb, even if not independently so. Is there any stage in the process at which life is not present? The mother's egg is alive in the sense of viable, as is the father's sperm that triggers the process of development of the fetus. When does this combination become *me*? As soon as the DNA sequences have combined and the first cell divides? All of the genetic instructions to build my body are present by this stage. All that happens from that point on is the addition of food.

Life, then, is undoubtedly a property that we have. We are alive but we are not "life." The property is one shared with everything from slime molds to mosquitoes and monkeys and we probably consider we are rather more than all of these. Science has taught us that all have one thing in common, namely DNA (or RNA) with specific genetic sequences determining what form the being will take. But we are not our genes or DNA. These are themselves nothing more than sets of instructions for converting food into forms more suited for use by the feeding organism – all very clever, unquestionably, but not *me*.

The third level of being according to the Sheath model is the mental realm – awareness of the environment and the ability to respond to it selectively. The plant responds automatically, moving toward light for example. We say that it does such things unconsciously, that it is not conscious of its surroundings. An animal, on the other hand, has some limited capability to choose how to interact and exhibits far more complex behavior – moving, foraging, sleeping and seeking a mate. This awareness is a different order of activity from that of plants. It can be lost in deep sleep or under anesthetic, in which circumstances the animal reverts to a plant-like behavior. Nevertheless, the animal's behavior is usually classed as instinctive, meaning that it is determined genetically or through mimicking its parents rather than through deliberate choice.

If a hungry tiger is presented with a choice between a deer and a leafy tree, there is no question as to the outcome. If the same choices are given to a hungry elephant, the outcome will be different but equally predictable. Animals behave according to their natures which, barring the interference by drugs or disease with their brain mechanisms, will always be the same in similar circumstances.

With man, something additional to animal qualities seems to have been introduced. Our behavior is not quite so predictable. It appears that we can take account of many variables and exercise reason to make conscious choices between many possible courses of action. Although we may act in a particular way at one time, we may act in a quite different way at another and the explanations for this may not be apparent to an observer and sometimes not even to ourselves.

Moreover, we are very much aware of ourselves as conscious entities and are able to observe and investigate this phenomenon of self-consciousness. This is the fourth level of being. We are able to make what we call moral decisions and act in ways that are apparently contrary to our self-interest. Such altruistic behavior is not usually associated with animals. Where it has been observed in them, it is perhaps better explained as instinctive but being in the best interest of the species rather than of the individual. Certainly, such behavior could not be argued as being the result of conscious deliberation and reasoned argument. In reported cases of dogs saving their master at the expense of their own life, there is an extreme of devotion perhaps. Or maybe, it is simply that the master is the provider of shelter and food and, if he goes, there will be neither. Animals are neither religious nor philosophical; they are lacking the equipment – namely the intellect – that enables these occupations.

Whatever it is that differentiates man from the animals can apparently be temporarily lost or permanently absent in some individuals and, just as an animal may lose consciousness and then behave like a plant, man without his intellect is said to behave like an animal. Conversely, some men seem to possess this quality to a high degree, enabling them to excel in their chosen field, whether in philosophical enquiry or in production of works of art.

Whereas the animal is limited by a nature that it has no power to alter, man has the capacity to overcome his perceived limitations and strive towards a distant goal. An animal that is hungry now will eat as soon as an opportunity is presented. Man can choose to reject something that will provide temporary enjoyment or satisfaction, deciding instead to hold out for some greater happiness in the future. In this, he may well be deluding himself, as was discussed earlier, but this is his apparent choice.

There is one final level according to the model and for most of us this will be in the realm of theory for the moment. It is the state of mind of the mystic or meditator when total stillness is reached. One is conscious but without any object of consciousness; the mind a complete blank without thought or emotion; simply and completely peaceful. It is the condition of *samadhi* or *nirvana*, which may last for moments, hours or even days but inevitably does come to an end. In the model, it is called the sheath of bliss. But because it is a state perceived by I-the-observer, it cannot be what I really am and, according to the Sherlock Rule, it must be eliminated too, pleasant though it is for the few able to experience it.

These, then, constitute the five sheaths that cover up our true nature. (Note that "cover up" is only a metaphor – it is not really like this.) Once they have been removed, or perhaps surmounted is a better word, who we really are is able to shine forth.

The *real* Self

It may seem unlikely at first sight that we should not know who we really are but the process of attachment and identification described above is so instantaneous and tenacious that we really do think that we are our bodies or our emotions or some other manifestation. We rarely if ever get around to thinking that something quite different might lie behind the appearance.

There is a classic story used to illustrate this (quoted from Ref. 46). It is usually referred to as the story of the tenth man. On the face of it, it is a very silly and obvious story with nothing useful to tell us. But, although you will have no difficulty understanding it, it is likely that the full import will elude you initially. When you truly appreciate it, it is really quite profound and sobering.

There is a party of ten men traveling together to a distant village in a remote and rugged area. They encounter a swollen river, which they are obliged to cross. They join hands and begin the perilous crossing but inevitably they lose their footing in the strong current and have to swim. Much later and wetter, they reassemble on the opposite bank. As each counts the number of men who have arrived, they can only find nine and conclude that one of their number has drowned.

As they are bemoaning their loss, a monk passes by and asks them what the matter is. They explain and, quickly assessing the situation, he recognizes their mistake. He asks them to line up and, taking a stick, he hits the first man once, the second twice and so on down the line, counting out the number aloud each time. Reaching the end, he hits the last man ten times and calls out "ten." What had happened, of course, is that each man had counted the others but forgotten to count himself, and so had only reached nine.

The reason for the total number is significant, each standing for an element in the makeup of Man. Note that this is as it was understood in ancient times – don't let any modern scientific hang-up about this distract you from the fundamental profundity of the story. The first nine are made up of the five elements of so-called gross matter – earth, water, air, fire and ether – together with the four subtle elements of mind – essentially all of the aspects that have just been covered above. The whole point of the story, however, is that we always forget the tenth, which is, of course, the true "I" or Self.

The ultimate mistake that is made, the cause of all of our false assumptions about ourselves and the consequent origin of all of our suffering is this process of taking ourselves to be something that we are not. We form false ideas about ourselves, thinking for example that we are a body, a mind or a role. We might say "I am a teacher." The "I am" part of this sentence is real. No one has any doubt that they exist even if, like Descartes, they should doubt everything else. But the "teacher" or whatever other attribution we might make is false. It is only a role that we play for some part of our lives. Our problems begin when we mix up the two.

One idea that has been used to help appreciate the nature of our Self a little better is that of a witness. If we avoid being caught up with any of the objects, thoughts or emotions that we are aware of, we can just observe them in a detached way. Since we can see them, we cannot be them. We are in a sense standing back, aloof from them all, aware of them in an objective sense while we are the subject. Of course, this is just an interim way of thinking about things since the notion of a witness ultimately turns out itself to be yet another superimposition.

The problem is that we are always looking outside of ourselves. The very nature of our senses is to point outwards. They collect information from the world, filter it using the built-in mechanisms provided by millions of years of evolution, and present it to the mind and intellect for analysis and assessment. But this very mechanism forever prevents us from seeing any reality. Even at a gross level, if we come out of a forest and suddenly see a tiger running towards us, we are not going to notice the beautiful rare flower on the ground nearby. Evolution forces us to notice what is going to ensure propagation of the species. The presentation of our senses is just that – a few relevant aspects chosen by evolution. We can never see things as they really are.

In the Gospel according to St Mark, Chapter 8, verse 35, Jesus is reported to have said: *"For whosoever will save his life shall lose it; but whosoever shall lose his life for my sake (and the gospel's) the same shall save it."* (I have put the reference to "gospels" in brackets. Clearly Jesus could not have referred to these since they were not written until long after his death. It is a good example of the way that the gospel writers distorted his words for their own benefit.) "Life" here, I suggest, means "ego"; "my sake" refers to the true Self. Those who persist in living their lives according to the credo of "*I* want; *I* matter" etc. miss the mark completely – this is the meaning of the word "sin." It is those who forego the ego in search of the true Self who find meaning and ultimate resolution in their lives. And they apparently find happiness, too...

The background of experience

I am not any of the things that I can perceive, feel or think. This worldly manifestation is appearing for my delectation as it were. I am merely the witness of it. I may appear to *have* a body but I can never say that I *am* the body. I am also not the mind, intellect or memory and I am not a person. I simply am. I am the Consciousness that, as a result of ignorance, gets identified with this body and mind etc.

But "you" can say exactly the same! *You* are not your body, mind and so on; *you* are the Consciousness that is identified with them. And of course it is now but a small step to ask about the relationship between these Consciousness-es. What relationship? There is no relationship, because there is only one Consciousness! This Consciousness is all that there is; the rest is simply an appearance which, in our ignorance, we mistake for something separate.

The best way to think about the nature of reality or Consciousness is as a background for all of the apparent manifestations of the phenomenal universe. We recognize the usual

three states of consciousness of waking, dreaming and deep
sleep. Paradoxically to the Western mind, deep sleep is closest to
our true nature, when there is no identification of any sort. Waking
and dreaming are very similar and our waking knowledge of the
dream state can give us an insight into the illusory character of
waking itself.

You might not have seen but will certainly be aware of the
Mount Rushmore memorial in South Dakota, where the heads of
four presidents are carved into the rock. Upon first looking at
something like this, one is initially struck by the faces themselves.
It is only later that there is the realization that not only are they
made out of rock but they are actually part of the cliff itself. There
is not actually anything other than rock in the entire thing. In the
same way, our ultimate nature is the background for the three states
of consciousness. I am awake, I dream and I go to sleep. It is in the
same "I" that these take place, though there will be the separate
appearance of a waking ego and a dream ego.

It will be explained in chapter 9 how reality and our real Self
are one and the same thing (so if you are unable to accept anything
that is being said in the rest of this chapter, wait until you have read
that before rejecting it). There is only this reality, Self, Absolute or
God – there is nothing else. The dawning of awareness of this truth
is called enlightenment or Self-realization. It is our real condition
now but not one that can be known objectively (since there are no
objects). It is possible to gain an intellectual appreciation and we,
the ego, can follow a notional spiritual path that can lead us
towards that realization.

But what is the nature of the reality seen by one who is
enlightened as opposed to how we presently see things? Well, it

is somewhat analogous to the way that an adult will see a magic trick compared to the way that a child views it. When the child sees the magician making someone disappear, she may well believe that this is actually happening. Although we may not be able to explain how it is done, nevertheless we know that it is an illusion. Similarly, we now look around us and believe that we see other people and separate objects. After Self-realization, the same visual scene is presented but it is now known irrevocably that the apparent separateness is an illusion. For the sake of convenience in thinking or speaking, we must use names to refer to specific forms of this appearance but the literal truth is that there is no separation at all.

The mind, too, is just as much a part of the illusion as is the world that it perceives. It has already been pointed out that the ego does not actually exist. The whole idea of my becoming enlightened and then knowing reality is a fiction. Both before and after, there is only ever the one reality. This is the ultimate paradox and one that is not soluble at the level of the mind. It is as if one of the characters in our dream were to wake up from the dream. From the context of the waking state, this is an illusion and makes no real sense.

And so, in the end we come full circle, back to where we began but with a radical new perspective. In a sense, we *are* the body and mind except that it is *all* bodies and *all* minds. There is no separation. There has never been any creation or birth and there will never be any death. There is nothing that we are not. There is no duality. There is awareness of all of this but no longer an "I" that is aware of it.

And this puts an entirely different complexion upon death. At first sight, most people would think that our fear of death is one of the most significant motivators in life. We are constantly concerned about our health. Some people have difficulty forming relationships because they are afraid of losing the other person. And we would all like to achieve something that we believe to be worthwhile before we die. All of this becomes irrelevant once we recognize that it is only bodies that die and that no one ever "does" anything. Who we really are is eternal; there are no "others."

The truth hidden within

Rudyard Kipling, in his address to The Royal College of Surgeons in February 1923, told the following story:

"There is a legend which has been transmitted to us from the remotest ages. It has entered into many brains and colored not a few creeds. It is this: Once upon a time, or rather, at the very birth of Time, when the Gods were so new that they had no names, and Man was still damp from the clay of the pit whence he had been digged, Man claimed that he, too, was in some sort a deity. The Gods were as just in those days as they are now. They weighed his evidence and decided that Man's claim was good – that he was, in effect, a divinity, and, as such, entitled to be freed from the trammels of mere brute instinct, and to enjoy the consequence of his own acts. But the Gods sell everything at a price. Having conceded Man's claim, the legend goes that they came by stealth and stole away this godhead, with intent to hide it where Man should never find it again. But that was none so easy. If they hid it anywhere on Earth, the Gods foresaw that Man, the inveterate hunter – the father, you might say, of all hunters – would leave no stone unturned nor wave unplumbed till he had recovered it. If they concealed it among themselves, they feared that Man might in the end batter his way up even to the skies. And, while they were all thus at a stand, the wisest of the Gods, who afterwards became the God Brahm, said, "*I* know. Give it to me!" And he closed his hand upon the tiny unstable light of Man's stolen godhead, and when that great Hand opened again, the light was gone. "All is well," said Brahm. "I have hidden it where Man will never dream of looking for it. I have hidden it inside Man himself."

This, then, is a metaphor for our present condition. We are looking everywhere outside of ourselves for happiness, truth, meaning etc. It never occurs to us to look inside or that we might already have the answers to all of these questions. There are many other stories to illustrate this situation. One of these concerns a thief who followed a rich merchant onto an overnight train journey and shared his carriage. The merchant was returning from a successful business trip and was carrying a considerable sum of money from his sales.

The thief knew that the merchant had the money secreted about his belongings somewhere so he went early to the bathroom that evening and then retired to his bunk and pretended to sleep. As soon as the merchant left the carriage to use the bathroom himself, the thief jumped out of his bunk and searched through the man's luggage and clothes. He was skilled in his profession and had no difficulty unlocking the cases and, in a very short time, had efficiently examined everything minutely – without finding any large sum of money or anything else of great value.

By the time that the merchant had returned, the thief was back in his bed apparently still asleep. But he did not sleep at all that night, as he lay awake worrying and wondering where the money had been hidden. As they were preparing to leave the train the next day, the thief turned to the merchant and confessed that he had been following him solely to steal his money. He explained how he had searched for it but failed to find anything and asked if the merchant would put him out of his misery and tell him where it had been hidden. The merchant then made his own confession. He had been perfectly aware of the other's intentions and had acted accordingly. He then reached over to the bunk and extracted a wallet of banknotes from underneath the thief's own pillow...

We, too, go through our lives thinking and acting like thieves, looking to steal things of value from the people and events around us when we already have all the "money" we could possibly want. We desire external objects and hope to find happiness in attaining them. We continually look everywhere else but within ourselves. If we could only do that, we would discover that we are already full-filled with happiness. It is the very act of looking outside of ourselves all of the time that prevents us from ever finding true happiness. Happiness is what remains when all of the searching ceases and we are left with our Self, which is perfect happiness. What you might think you want is due to a perceived lack or limitation. In reality, your true nature is without any limits. Therefore, you really need and should want nothing because you already have everything.

There is one thing in common with all of the various pursuits that we looked at earlier, which people follow in order to find happiness. Whether it is in objects or through involvement in work or play, in a spouse or child, following a dangerous sport or taking drugs, in contemplation or meditation or any of the thousand and one other things that you might think of – they all take us away from the ego with its perceived limitations. They "take us out of ourselves" or make us "forget ourselves" for a while. And whilst the ego and its identifications are forgotten, the Self is free to simply be and enjoy itself in whatever happens to be going on at the time. The Self is always there, pure, free and blissful but we cover it up. We believe that we are lacking something and therefore feel miserable, spending all our efforts trying to do something in order to find the happiness that is already our own nature.

In fact, we have no problems at all. The body might be less than perfect. It might even be ill. Our memories deteriorate inexorably as the body grows older. The brain becomes poorer at solving problems and its reaction times slow. But we are none of these. The problems relate to body and mind and not to who we really are. We have no such limitations. Once the fundamental problem of identification has been dissolved, all other so-called problems disappear.

8. How can we be happy now?

There is one final area to be investigated before we move on to the denouement and ask about the nature of reality itself. This involves looking at what we can actually do in order to realize for ourselves the truth of what is being said here. You may be somewhat nonplussed at this statement since we have previously discussed how we do nothing and are unable freely to choose to do anything anyway. But there is no problem here. The chain of apparent cause and effect in your life led you to buy (borrow or steal) this book and the ideas expressed will be having their own impact upon your way of thinking. Depending upon how ingrained your habits are, the flexibility of your neuronal pathways if you like, you are able to take on board new ideas and effectively modify your previous behavior and beliefs. But there is no choice or doing involved – it simply happens. There is no contradiction here of what has gone before.

Given this then, there are a number of practices that may be taken up which will eventually have an effect upon your outlook. Essentially they are mechanisms for bringing us into the present. I have already mentioned how it is that most of us, for most of the time, live in an illusory world of past or future. (The illusion itself is in the present of course.) In the past we relive old memories, suffer disappointments and resentment. In the future we imagine what might happen and suffer consequential anxiety and tension. In actuality, there is only ever the present and, in the present, there *are* no problems.

Read, listen and reflect

What needs to happen is that we effectively awaken from the delusion from which we are suffering, dispel the ignorance and simply see this apparent world for what it really is. But, as you no doubt appreciate, this is as if one of the characters in your dream were to tell you that you are not really a starving beggar but the king. The fact remains that you are still in the dream and probably treating much of what has been said as far less plausible than your everyday experience. After all, you get up, eat meals, go to work and watch TV every day. You are used to all that stuff and have no trouble accepting it as reality. When this is all questioned and it is suggested that your entire life to date has been an illusion, it is understandable that there should be some skepticism.

We cannot actually see the world as an illusion. The realized man still sees the same appearance as we do but simply knows that it is not a separate, independent reality, in the same way that we know the lady is not really being sawn in half, if you recall the metaphor of the magician used earlier. What is needed is for us to undergo this shift in the way that we think about everything. We normally think that, if we are not to awaken from our sleep naturally, then an external event is needed, such as someone shaking us or an alarm clock going off. But it *is* possible for an event within the dream itself to serve this function. Suppose you are dreaming that you are in a jungle being chased by a lion and you are growing weary. If you turn around and the lion charges straight at you and pounces, it is very likely that you will wake up!

Unfortunately, it is most unlikely that this scenario would work analogously in our waking situation. If we were able to surrender totally, we might realize our true nature – though there would be little appreciation of the fact through the medium of a body that was in the process of being eaten! Nevertheless, we can prepare the ground. It is possible that reading this book may act as the impetus for further study. The more that you understand the essence of what is being said, the greater the possibility that a metaphorical lion will tip the balance and devour the mindset that is covering the truth.

Naturally, you may still be somewhat skeptical about this. You cannot expect to read something as seemingly radical as this and be able fully to appreciate it immediately. Even if you were able to discuss things at length with someone who had realized this truth, who could address each of your doubts in turn, it would still be some time before the import and consequences began to sink in.

The problem is that your present beliefs are so entrenched. After all, you have been living with them essentially all of your life. You cannot help but view the world and yourself through all of these existing concepts. It is as if you were wearing a pair of colored spectacles. If the glass in the spectacles is green, it is inevitable that the world will appear green. If I tell you that it is really not like this, all that you need to do to confirm what I am saying is to remove the spectacles. Unfortunately, removing your concepts is a much more gradual, difficult and painful process.

The intended effect of your reading what has gone before is that you will want to find out more about these ideas and the philosophy that underlies them, that you will feel that they might provide the sort of meaning that you have been looking for in your lives. I will mention its origin just briefly here. It is called "Advaita" which, perhaps unsurprisingly, means "not two" (in Sanskrit). It derives from the ancient Eastern texts called the

Upanishads but was systematized as a philosophy in around the 8th century AD by someone called Shankara. I am not going to say anything more about it here because the idea of this book is to use simple logic and appeals to common sense. Then you use your own experience to validate the ideas that are presented without reference to obscure spiritual sources or religions that you will not, in all probability, have heard of. My website at www.advaita.org.uk will forward you to all that you might wish to find out on the subject if you decide to pursue it.

You will rightly have recognized that the aims that have been advocated are spiritual ones and you may wonder whether such an approach is reasonable. In today's society, spiritual pursuits of any kind not overtly religious tend to be equated with "new age" beliefs, in derogatory quotation marks. In the minds of many, this means an unreal, utopian lifestyle based upon pseudo-scientific and ultimately nonsensical ideas. Most people have a view of the world being full of poverty and misery and self-righteously criticize any spiritually minded people who talk about, and supposedly seek, perfection whilst tacitly ignoring the real life going on all around us.

In fact, many of those who help others are often intent only on themselves. This may be in the sense of making themselves appear virtuous, e.g. the rich donating to charities or large companies spending relatively trivial amounts on those peoples whose land they are destroying. At the individual level, few act totally without thought for themselves or without expectation of future reward unless it is in respect of friends or family.

A hierarchy of types of action can be specified in this sense of helping others. The action involving the least effort and of least value for the recipient is one of giving money. Next in the hierarchy is the donation of some material possession of your own such as, for example, giving your jacket to a beggar. Here, the loss is immediately noticeable, whereas the coins are probably forgotten the next minute... once the feeling of self-righteousness has worn off. The next highest in value is the effective giving of your own person. This would mean spending time physically helping the recipient. Examples are those who work in charity shops or deliver meals-on-wheels to the elderly and disabled. The most valuable help that you can give, however, is to follow a path to Self-realization. Once one is able act in full knowledge of the truth of the Self, then everyone benefits and people will come to you for help; you do not have to do anything. A more mundane way of putting this is that you cannot really help others until you can help yourself.

It is certainly true that you will find it difficult to follow up these ideas. Not because of any intrinsic difficulty or because the material is especially hard to find but because of habit. The illusory and mistaken view of yourself and the world will continue to be confirmed by everyone and everything around you. If you attempt to discuss the claims of this book, your listeners are likely to ridicule you – and your understanding is unlikely yet to be sufficiently sound to resist them. Society, science and even much of what claims to be religion have a vested interest in perpetuating their variants of the illusion. As soon as you have finished this book and filed it away, the ideas will begin to fade, likely to be relegated to the merely interesting or even the weird-but-irrelevant.

When ideas contravene existing beliefs, it is our natural tendency to ignore them so as to maintain the status quo. You must ask yourself, if tempted to do this, whether the status quo is acceptable. If you are already totally happy, satisfied that you have both meaning and purpose in your life, then why should you bother investigating further? But then, in that case, why are you reading this book?

Confronting issues such as these can certainly be disquieting but only by doing so can we resolve them and reach understanding. They will not go away by ignoring them.

Direct your attention

If attention is given exclusively to a task in which an end result is sought, then there is far more likelihood of achieving those results because distracting thoughts and feelings have been eliminated. More significantly, the ego that wants the result is temporarily forgotten. This attitude and practice can be applied to all aspects of life, from the trivial to the long term; from making a cup of coffee to working towards promotion at work or getting to know the girl in the next office.

Someone may have what everyone regards as a boring, repetitive job, which on the face of it offers not the slightest scope for originality or imagination. Most people in such a situation will simply learn the necessary movements until they become automatic and then switch off. They will continue to perform the motions but with their minds elsewhere, whether dreaming of holidays, eyes wandering around the room looking for stimulation or mentally solving differential equations. Their attention will be unfocussed on the task and they will not feel at all involved in what they are doing – most likely, they will claim to be bored out of their minds. But it is possible to make even the most mundane of activities into a challenge and become involved, whether by trying to perfect one's movements, turning them into a ballet or simply trying to minimize the elapsed time to perform a sequence.

It is easier to give our attention to something that we deem to be interesting but, with practice, the reverse can also happen – interest can be generated by giving our attention to an unwelcome task. Prisoners in solitary confinement have retained their sanity by devising intellectual games, mentally writing poetry or trying to picture scenes in the cracks and marks on a blank wall. Through determinedly giving their full attention to such tasks, a sense of purpose is retained and the mind kept active.

Attention to something external also takes us away from awareness of our selves. We become less self-conscious, which means less egocentric and therefore more truly our real self, and thus happier. Attention can even reduce body consciousness to the level where we are no longer aware of pain. I always remember a cross-country race at school. I was performing well and fully intent simply on the race. My parents were watching and I was determined to do my best. I even put on a sprint for the last hundred yards or so and managed to overtake another runner. As soon as I passed the finish line, I collapsed in exhaustion. But it was only after a minute or so that I realized that my heel was painful. Looking down, I saw that a large blister had formed and burst, with blood all over my sock. I had not noticed this at all whilst running. Pain is an evolutionary development to draw our attention to the body when it is injured so that we may take appropriate action. But we are not the body and, if we are otherwise engaged on what is deemed to be a more important activity, pain can be ignored.

Attention is also related to habit and conditioning. There is always a tendency to act as we have done in the past, making the same mistakes or failing because the situation is not quite the same as it was last time. If we have learnt how to perform a particular activity, it may be easier to repeat the actions mechanically, without attention, leaving our minds free to daydream but this can never be responsive to the unique demands of the present situation. Attention can only be directed to a task if the mind is free of thoughts, available to assess the needs and make appropriate decisions in clarity. Absence of attachment to ideas in mind is tantamount to absence of ego, detachment from a vested interest in the outcome.

It is the same principle as was mentioned in respect of desire and happiness. Whilst the desire is there, we feel unfulfilled, sensing a lack. At the moment that the desired object is obtained, we feel one with it; the sense of separation between it and ourselves is temporarily dissolved. The sense of a separate ego is momentarily lost and happiness, our true natural state, reigns for a while... until the next desire comes along.

It follows from this that losing the ego permanently would bring about happiness in everything that we do. It is the ego that habitually gets in the way. This is all very paradoxical, of course – I want to be happy but, while there is an "I" that wants this, there is not going to be any lasting happiness. The way to act is not to invest any egotistical element into a particular outcome. We must act simply in response to the needs of the situation without seeking any result, whether for ourselves or another. Simply empty the mind completely of all thoughts and let the attention rest on the point at which the work is being done.

Live in the present

There is a story about an arrow-maker, who was so intent on sharpening the point of the arrow on which he was working that he completely failed to hear the noise of the king's procession that was passing by outside of his house. This extremity of attention is equivalent to the meditative mind giving full attention to a mantra. Its character is quite different from that of the attention in the daydream or in the reading of escapist fiction. There, the attention is taken away from us and we are lost in a world of imagination.

In the case of the arrow maker, full attention is given to the point where the action is taking place and it is given lightly and without effort. But the skill required to achieve the necessary level of perfection leaves no attention spare for attending to unrelated things such as the passing procession. It is a level of consciousness without any of the clouding from irrelevant sensations and perceptions. Consciousness is undivided and the ego is quite absent. Whenever such moments occur, *I* am not giving the attention. Hopefully, it is becoming clearer now that it is the absence of ego that is the key to a sense of purpose and happiness and its presence is the lock that prevents our access to them.

It is the fact that I am no longer thinking about myself and whether things are going as I wish etc., that is significant. To put it in mystical terms (that will become much less mystical as you read the final section of this book), you become one with the arrow point if you are an arrow maker or with the rock face if you are a climber. T. S. Eliot speaks of it (*Four Quartets*) in reference to listening to music: "...*music heard so deeply that it is not heard at all, but you are the music while the music lasts*". Our identity is lost and we merge temporarily with the natural happiness of our true self. Afterwards, we erroneously attribute our experience to the music. At the moment of happiness, there is no objective music nor an enjoyer of it.

It is worth noting in passing that it is no coincidence that many of the activities in which this happens are what one might consider dangerous. This is simply because life-threatening situations make it that much easier to give undivided attention, raising one's awareness to rare peaks of intensity. At the opposite extreme, when attention is diffused or wandering aimlessly, we are aware of ourselves, not knowing what to do or wanting to do something else and the feeling is typically one of boredom.

The other aspect of this experience is that it takes place in the present. This might seem a trite observation but the fact of the matter is that much of our attention seeks to travel outside of this necessary limitation. Though it is an unavoidable fact that there is only ever the present moment, nevertheless we insist on reminiscing or agonizing over what is now past, reliving moments of happiness or wishing that we had acted differently. And we plan incessantly, considering "what might happen if" and debating whether this or that would be the optimum course of action. Frequently our minds are indulging in these futile activities even whilst we are supposed to be concentrating upon what we are doing – and we wonder why we have accidents! If you have any doubts about the truth of all of this, just reflect for a moment that you tend to say that you are "thinking" only when you are not actively involved in doing something. It is when the attention is not under control and directed to a specific activity that the mind takes over and we end up indulging in circling thoughts.

This inability to give or to control attention is itself very frustrating. In extreme conditions it can be so disruptive that the so-called experts classify it as a mental illness. In children, Attention Deficit Hyperactivity Disorder (ADHD) prevents learning and causes problems not only for the children themselves but also for their family, teachers and anyone else that has to interact with them. The most severe manifestation is in schizophrenics who cannot even control their own thoughts and cannot give their attention to a single thing. Everything crowds in upon them, taking over their lives and eliminating the possibility for any sort of enjoyment.

Thus it is that people often miss the opportunity for enjoying themselves here and now because their minds are effectively not in the present; they are unable to direct their attention. They are dreaming or regretting, revisiting or inwardly debating something quite unrelated to the present activity or the data currently entering our senses. If we are always planning and looking forward to a time in the future when we think we will be happy, it is hardly surprising that we are never happy *now* – and now is the only time when we can be happy. In fact, that sentence is worth repeating and underlining – Now is the only time when we can be happy!

It is understandable that, if our attention is partly directed towards memories or imagined futures, then the experience here in the present must be diminished. It is during those periods when we are totally in the present that we report feelings of being intensely alive, seeing everything with unnatural clarity and brilliant color and so on. It is a dire condemnation of our normal state of awareness that this happens so infrequently.

Paradoxical as it might seem, the working hours of most people provide them with more opportunity than do the leisure hours for constructive involvement, forgetting of ego and therefore positive enjoyment. Work usually has goals and rules, often provides challenges that have to be met, has opportunities for creative effort and provides feedback. Conversely, sitting in front of the television or other passive ways of spending one's free time offer little in the way of any of these things and are very likely to lead to negative feelings of listlessness and dissatisfaction. If we sit around doing nothing, we simply become bored.

We need to put effort into our recreation too if this word is to satisfy its literal meaning of re-creation. It is acts of creation that give positive rewards – making music instead of listening to it, playing sport instead of watching it on TV and so on. It is those people with constructive and creative hobbies who report being happy in their leisure time, while the ones who sit around idly by themselves merely feel apathetic.

It might, then, seem to be a reasonable aim simply to live one's life in the present, never dwelling upon what has gone nor imagining what might come. This is how we typically think though – and miss the point yet again. If we are "aiming" to do this, it is again something in the future – we have to do it now!

Be detached

This might be seen as the opposite of involvement and the freely given attention of the arrow maker. But it is not as simple as this. Along with involvement comes the ever-present threat of attachment, which we now recognize as the source of most of our problems. We can become attached to the enjoyment that results from a particular activity, such as drug taking. Or we can become attached to the outcome – an example of this would be only being able to enjoy playing a sport if we win. The arrow maker being attached to the results of his action would be an example of this. He might be intent not simply in letting his attention rest upon the point where the action is taking place but upon making this point the sharpest that has ever been produced. Here is the ego again, ever-ready to leap in and take over, as soon as our vigilance is reduced.

It is human nature to have a vested interest in the outcome of events. Genetic heritage ensures that the inclination of the animal will be to ensure its survival. It will naturally choose whichever option maximizes the possible benefit to its body-mind or those of its immediate family or society. Accordingly, if the attention is not directed at the moment of action, the response will inevitably be pre-programmed or habitual and there will be attachment to the outcome.

Detachment, on the other hand, is the attitude of having no interest in the outcome, simply acting in accordance with the perceived need, deriving no pleasure or disappointment from the result. It arises out of the knowledge that who-we-really-are is totally unaffected by either. If we respond in the moment with full attention, then the outcome will be optimal – we need not feel elated at a favorable outcome or dejected if the result is deemed by others to be bad. What others think makes no difference. As the classic Indian work, the *Bhagavad Gita*, tells us, freedom lies in not being attached to the fruit of action.

Detachment means that we are not taken in by the thoughtless views of others, by advertising and fashion. In the presence of detachment and stillness, discrimination can operate and what really matters in any given situation can be clearly seen.

Ultimately, this can manifest as total indifference to the false values imposed upon things by others; seeing things as they really are. For example, a designer dress is merely a status symbol, justifying its high price merely on the basis of exclusivity and is in no way related to functionality.

When developed to a high level, we can become a witness of all that takes place, whether in the outside world or within our own mind. We are not the doer, enjoyer or thinker and we can simply watch all of these things taking place in the full knowledge that we are not doing any of them. It is difficult to behave like this because we never have before. It is almost certain that you will remain highly skeptical even if your mind does not resort to outright ridicule. But try simply watching yourself making a cup of coffee. Do it now!

Get up out of the chair and follow your normal procedure of making a coffee (or tea or fruit juice) but with the following crucial difference: Empty your mind of thoughts to begin with and give your full attention to each minute action. Look, now the legs are walking into the kitchen; the hand is moving towards the cupboard and opening it, etc. At each stage, just watch without interfering. It is all taking place but you are simply the witness of everything. It is possible to see this for yourself without the slightest difficulty.

Meditate

Meditation is the epitome of freely given but controlled attention and, following on from the logic of what has just been discussed, it is able to achieve complete elimination of ego from consciousness and bring with that the experience of complete tranquility. The usual state of our mind is one of dominion by thought. Our attention wanders, is caught by something and a thought is triggered. This, in turn, sets in motion an avalanche of associated ideas and memories, reminiscences, worries, anticipation, imagination… you name it! This process can continue for a long time, often until it is checked by our noticing something else, hearing a voice addressing us or whatever it might be and then a new chain is begun.

We sometimes feel that we can direct this process – when studying or working towards a specific end, for example but this is really only a matter of degree. When we pick up a book and open it at a chosen page and begin to read, the mechanism is set off on a predetermined track. It is likely to remain on the rails as long as no stimulus of greater interest comes along. But it is still very much an automatic activity, programmed and practiced until we are able to perform it without too much distraction. We cannot really claim to be in control. It would be much more accurate to admit that, for most of the time in our lives, the mind or the thoughts in it control us. We are bounced from desire to fear, from elation to resentment, as first one thought then another attains dominance.

We only really achieve a sense of freedom when the mind becomes silent and there are no thoughts at all. Most people rarely experience this and some may even doubt that it is possible. A few even equate the idea of no-mind with death and fear such a state. Note that this is not to say that thoughts are bad *per se* – indeed, it is simply the nature of the mind to think. The problem is: who is in charge? We are not the mind, as has been established earlier, so it cannot be right for it to exercise dominion over us. We would like always to be in charge, using the mind as required for the tool that it is. Also, instead of forever looking outwards towards the supposed objects and pleasures of the world-appearance, it would be valuable to direct the mind inwards to consider our own nature and use it to understand the ideas that are being presented in this book. Meditation is often represented as being a technique for reducing stress, improving the ability to concentrate, making one more effective in life and so on. And so it is. But all of these purported aims are egotistical ones – I want to perform better, be healthier and achieve some desired aim – and they all miss the point completely. The true purpose of meditation is to prime the mind for self-destruction. All spiritual paths aim to dissolve the ego so that the true Self may be realized, removing the ignorance that prevents this recognition. Meditation is a valuable aid in this because the ignorance is in the mind. In a sense, ignorance *is* the mind; mind and ego are effectively the same thing. The Self is mistakenly identified with body, mind, intellect or soul as a result of ideas in the mind that obscure the truth. Once all of this mental clutter has been removed and there is only clarity and silence, there is an opportunity simply to realize the truth.

Differentiate between the pleasant and the good

Pleasure and happiness were discussed earlier and it was noted that the former is invariably only a transient phenomenon whose complement, pain, is never far away. Happiness on the other hand is an aspect of our true nature and is always there to be found if only we would stop looking in the wrong direction. This is the eternal dichotomy between what has been called the pleasant and the good. Those who pursue the former are doomed to a life of disappointments and ultimately perceived failure. Only the path of the good can lead to our truly desired goal of happiness and fulfillment, in which we realize our true nature.

We are used to looking elsewhere for purpose and satisfaction in our lives. We desire material objects, want to associate with attractive or famous people. We want better jobs, more money and more time to follow our hobbies or watch television (excuse the judgmental view that watching television is not a hobby!). Our lives are a continual looking outwards, away from ourselves, both for entertainment and meaning.

Our happiness is intrinsically concerned with who we are, not with what we think we might become. We will never find purpose or make sense of our lives, never find out who we really are, if we are always looking elsewhere. Everything outside is ostensibly (apologies for this qualification but all will be revealed in the next chapter) other than ourselves and we will not find any joy there. The very search presupposes that we are lacking something and need to look outside of ourselves in order to discover fulfillment. I.e. the premise of the search is based on error. The only end to be found from searching forever outside of ourselves is delusion and death. Such a search will only discover pleasure and pain in equal measure – this is the path of the pleasant.

We need to stop, turn away from the enticing but ultimately worthless baubles that beckon on all sides and start to look within, ask resolutely who we are and refuse to stop until we find the answer. The world is not what it seems to be. Its attractions are ephemeral and ultimately prove to be unreal. We may not yet fully understand this and we may well fail to achieve so-called enlightenment. But at least this search is founded in truth and our efforts will not be wasted. This is the path of the good – philosophy or love of truth.

The *Bhagavad Gita*, one of the greatest works of spiritual guidance, describes the path of the pleasant as one that is like nectar in the beginning but ultimately like poison. This can be seen clearly in an example such as drug addiction. Someone initially introduced to heroin no doubt experiences ecstatic pleasure, unlike any he has previously encountered. All too soon, however, he discovers that more and more is needed to bring about even moderate highs. Ultimately, he has to take the drug in order to avoid the pain of being without it. Although this is an extreme example, most of us will admit that we tend to choose those things that bring instant pleasure out of habit or attachment.

✳ In contrast, the path of the good is described as being like poison in the beginning but like nectar in the end. Initially, turning away from the attractions of the world is difficult and all spiritual disciplines are found initially to be tedious at the least. You would no doubt claim that finding two half-hour periods each day for meditation, for example, would be impossible! And yet, if such a path is undertaken with resolution, the seeming obstacles are eventually overcome and benefits are increasingly realized. And, of course, if the path is pursued to its final goal, the rewards are infinite. In order to make this choice, we need the benefit of wisdom and discriminating intellect acting out of clarity of thought rather than an automatic and dull reaction.

The seeker is never going to find the Self

There is unfortunately a very real problem with all of this, although again, paradoxically, there is no problem at all. We looked earlier at the process of identification, at all of the things that we usually think ourselves to be and how these beliefs are mistaken. And we moved on to talk about the Self that we truly are. Now of course we *are* this Self, already – how could we not be? Nothing we can ever do could take us towards (or away from) what we really are.

The problem is that, whilst we think that we are *not* the Self, and have to do some something to become it, we are continually turning away from this truth. It is like the man looking everywhere for his spectacles when they are actually pushed back on his own forehead. He is never going to find them whilst he is looking all over the house. Similarly, we are looking everywhere in the world for meaning, everywhere outside of ourselves in order to find ourselves and we are doomed to failure. It is only when we turn back, so to speak, and we look within that we can hope to succeed. Even then, we must drop all of our preconceptions and attachments; uncover all of the accumulated ignorance through which we normally look, before we can realize the truth. And that truth is an intuitive realization, a subjective "I am" and not an objective "I am *this.*"

What we really are cannot be perceived – we are not the perceiver. It cannot be felt or thought about – we are neither thoughts nor the thinker or feeler. We are beyond all of these; the mind and intellect are tools that we use. These tools cannot conceive of the one that uses them. A helpful metaphor is that of a torch. If you are in a totally dark room, you may use a torch to see most things. But the one thing that you will never be able to see with it (without being very devious and abusing the metaphor) is the battery that powers the torch.

There is not actually anything that we can *do* to realize this truth. We are trapped in our false beliefs and unable to take it in. And that reminds me of the story of the Professor and the

Zen teacher:

A professor of philosophy is visiting a Zen monastery in Japan and goes to visit the Zen master to ask for explanations about the teaching. The master invites him to take tea. The professor holds out his cup and the master pours the tea... and carries on pouring, until the tea is overflowing onto the floor.

"The cup is full," complains the professor, "it will not hold any more."

"Just so!" replies the master. "You, too, are like the cup. How can I explain anything to you when your mind is already full of what you consider to be the truth?"

We have to empty our minds of all of our preconceptions and start again from the beginning. And no one is suggesting that you simply fill it up again with ideas such as the ones in this book. You must test each new idea in your experience. Reflect upon all new concepts in the light of silence, quietly exposing them to the discrimination of your true intellect, not to the tired old arguments that others have used, no matter in what regard you might hold them.

What is being said here may seem new; it is not. On the contrary, it is ancient knowledge that has been conveniently forgotten by the materially minded West. As things stand, modern society is heading for a hedonistic hell, with individuals seeking more and more material possessions but finding less and less satisfaction in them. The evidence has been growing in the sociological surveys of the past twenty years – that way does not lead to happiness. But, driven by advertising and the incestuous demands of capitalism, we blindly follow the fashions and lose the purpose of action.

If we simply carry on as we are, then, we can be certain of the outcome. We will continue to be at the mercy of circumstance, elated by a transient pleasure at one minute, depressed and disillusioned by misfortune at the next. We will search in vain to find meaning or purpose in the ephemeral and temporal. Even if we could possess the whole world, what would be the point? The earth is doomed to be baked by the expanding sun in a paltry few billion years. And what is the significance of the earth and its surface life-forms in the context of the universe? Within this picture, any sense of purpose is only relative to that of our neighbors. Any larger picture rapidly loses its significance.

9. The nature of reality

If you have managed to read this far, you may well be wondering whether you made a wise decision in buying this book. Perhaps you were expecting that, by now, you would have some good ideas as to what are the important things in life and how to go about getting them. It may seem that all I have done is to destroy all of your existing, cherished beliefs and not replaced them with any suitable alternative, given that the idea that we are "Consciousness" probably still does not really make sense. If this is your concern then perhaps you had better stop reading now... because I have saved the most devastating part until the end, the part that completely demolishes the foundations of the traditional ways of thinking about life and what matters. If you are familiar with the work of philosophers such as Berkeley, Kant and Schopenhauer then what follows will, at least initially, be quite familiar to you. If not, it may come as a bit of a surprise. And for those who have encountered the Western teachings, the final aspects, more attributable to Eastern philosophers such as Adi Shankara and Atmananda Krishna Menon, may surprise even you!

It is necessary that we do look into this in some depth because it is not meaningful to make decisions about what really matters in the world if we don't have an understanding of what the world is. You can appreciate this by thinking for a moment of a very realistic dream you might have had. Suppose that you were driving along a country road and suddenly came upon an injured cyclist, apparently knocked off his bike by another motorist and left bleeding in the road. You recall passing a telephone kiosk a little way back and immediately turn around and drive back to it so that you can call for an ambulance. (How could you have forgotten your mobile?) As you get out of the car and walk to the kiosk, the telephone rings and... you wake up to the sound of the alarm clock.

Now, do you immediately get out of bed and call for an ambulance to go and rescue the cyclist? Now that you have awakened from the dream, whose content was entirely a product of your own mind, you recognize that there is no longer any need – the cyclist only existed in your imagination. Even "you", the driver of the car, never existed in reality.

In just the same way, before we can make truly justifiable decisions about what we should be doing with our lives, we need to be very certain about the reality of the various options. This might be as trivial as recognizing that some object that we think might bring us happiness will not do so if we actually manage to get it. At the other extreme though, perhaps we could effectively wake up from what we currently perceive as our normal waking existence and realize that it was just as much a dream as what we now think of as our dreaming sleep.

Stuff

Ever since man first had the luxury of being able to sit and think as opposed to having to find food or fight off adversaries for most of his waking life, he has probably found himself occasionally looking around and wondering what exactly it is that he sees. The earliest Greek philosophers, a couple of hundred years before Plato, were concerned with such things as discovering the primary constituent of matter and the governing principles of the universe. They asked themselves: "What is the nature of the universe?"

Heraclitus is one of the better known, famous for his

observation that the river that we step into for a second time is effectively not the same as the one into which we stepped the first time. The world has always and will always exist, he said, but "*was ever, is now, and ever shall be, an ever-living Fire*", constantly changing. Things that appear to be opposites are really just extremes of a single thing, like the north and south poles of a magnet. Our phenomenal world is in a constant state of flux and the key to understanding it is introspection, looking inwards to find ourselves where there is stability and changelessness. "*All things come out of one*," he said, "*and the one out of all things; but the many have less reality than the one, which is God.*" He was probably what we would now term a mystic and the few fragments of his writing that remain are obscure, to say the least! But these cryptic comments influenced later philosophers such as Hegel and Nietzsche, as well as others such as T. S. Eliot, whose wonderful poem the *Four Quartets* quotes him directly in several places.

A disciple of Heraclitus, called Cratylus, took the idea of continual change to its limits. He said that it was not even possible to hold a discussion since, by the time one came to answer a question, the person asking the question, the one answering and even the words and meanings would all have changed. So all he could do when asked something was wiggle a finger to indicate that he had heard... though whom he thought he was responding to is unclear.

Parmenides believed that our senses deceive us as regards the nature of objects. There are not *many* things but only the One, which is infinite and indivisible, present everywhere (and spherical!). He disagreed totally with Heraclitus, saying that there is *never* any change. There must *be* things, since we think of them and name them. Since we can do this at any moment, they must always exist. Conversely, it is simply not possible to think or speak of things that do not exist. The real always exists and is unchanging. That which changes must not exist and cannot be part of the real.

This is not an intuitive conclusion but, provides a very useful working definition of the word "real." For something to be *truly* real, it has to exist always and never change. After all, if it changes into something different it cannot have been real can it? Conversely, when we see things changing, what we perceived must only have been a moving shape or form, like a dream and not truly real. This idea is a very important one.

Aristotle asked: if we do not understand the nature of reality, how can we know how to act? We could live our entire lives on the assumption that there is no afterlife for example, seeking self-gratification and ignoring the feelings of others. If this turns out to be wrong we could be reborn as a cockroach or find ourselves burning in hell for the rest of eternity. And that ought to be a cause for concern, since the duration of this life is rather insignificant compared to that of eternity!

The pre-Socratic philosophers were trying to reduce the stuff of the world to something simple and ideally unitary. Thus Thales thought it was made of water, Anaximenes that it was air and Heraclitus fire. Others, such as Democritus, even anticipated the idea of atoms, believing that matter consisted of indivisible particles that were too small for us to see. But, as can be seen from the Heraclitus quotation above, they were not exactly materialists in the sense of someone like Hobbes. The latter would have us believe that there is only matter and that we ourselves are entirely mechanical. The former were searching for some unifying principle that we could equally well call God.

Is this a dagger I see before me?

Born some eighteen years before the death of Descartes, the Englishman John Locke believed that external objects had what he called primary qualities; these were aspects that could be measured scientifically such as length, mass, velocity and so on. Those aspects such as smell and taste, he called secondary qualities and he said that these were not intrinsic to the object itself (they could not be measured scientifically) but were simply a subjective interpretation in our mind, triggered by the primary qualities.

He said that we can only ever be aware of these qualities, which are effectively transactions between an actual object and ourselves as the subject. We cannot know anything about the matter itself, independent of these characteristics, nor of ourselves, independent of these experiences. Most importantly, the conclusions of this approach meant that we can never know any absolute truths about the universe, only develop possible hypotheses that seem to explain our observations. Once we accept this, we can stop wasting our time trying to understand things that are forever beyond our ken.

The Irish philosopher Bishop George Berkeley objected to Locke's classification of qualities into primary and secondary. He said that this would mean that our senses were unreliable; that reality was one thing while our senses told us something else. Such ideas could only lead us into doubt and skepticism. If the ordinary person saw that philosophers, who had devoted their lives to studying the nature of knowledge and reality, were coming up with ideas that were contradictory to all of their experience and common sense, it could only lead to atheism... all of which makes his own view of things somewhat amazing!

He showed that, if we accepted the view that all of our knowledge derives from experience then we are inevitably led to deny any objective reality to the world. We can only ever know anything via our senses. Locke had said that there were real objects possessing primary qualities but Berkeley argued that our awareness of primary is really no different from our awareness of the secondary qualities. We are only aware of form, size and motion and so on as a result of sight and touch, and these are ultimately only perceptions in our minds just the same.

That our perception is always subjective can be shown by the fact that our interpretation depends upon where we are and what we are doing at the time. We can easily misjudge the size of something if there is no known object in the vicinity with which to compare it. This is why the sun and moon appear so much larger when close to the horizon, with trees and buildings for comparison. If we ourselves are moving, we can mistake the degree to which another object is moving, as we know when we are in a train standing next to another in the station – when one begins to move we are initially unsure which it is. Everything about a supposed external object is in fact in our mind and there can never be any independent validation that it exists when we are not immediately aware of it.

It is pointless trying to argue that an object has certain qualities that we cannot perceive and that these are the *cause* of our perceptions since, by definition, this could never be proven. Furthermore, it would not make any sense to say that our ideas and impressions are *like* the supposed real object because we think that the object exists relatively unchanging over time whereas we know that our thoughts are transient and change frequently. We can only say that our sensations are *like* sensations, which only exist within living things. We cannot even imagine something with qualities other than those that we perceive existing alone without someone to perceive them. As soon as we imagine it, it is by definition an idea in our minds. And if qualities that we cannot perceive did exist, again by definition, we could never be aware of them.

Berkeley argued that all of this followed from the Empiricist assumption that knowledge derives from experience. Since that experience itself comes from sense data alone and these consist only of ideas in mind, we can only ever experience ideas and never any real objects. Everything that we perceive is an idea and ideas cannot exist outside of the mind. (This includes the brain itself, so that the brain is in the mind, not vice versa!) As he famously put it, "*to be is to be perceived.*"

Thus his claim was that there are only two elements to our perceptual experience: the perceiver and the ideas in mind that he perceives. There are no such things as material objects. This theory was called Immaterialism or Idealism – nothing to do with the pursuit of ideals but the theory that what is real is effectively contained within our minds as ideas. Most people find his claims fantastical to say the least, despite the fact that they are unable to find any obvious counter arguments. In fact, at the time, Berkeley believed his theory corresponded most clearly with common sense and said that it was held alike by ordinary men (the "vulgar") and philosophers.

But so-called objects in dreams seem perfectly real whilst we are still in the dream. It is only after we wake up that we accept that they were not. Furthermore this difference is not based upon the belief that dream objects are only in our minds whereas waking objects consist of *matter*. Our perception of the relative reality of waking objects is based upon such things as their seeming duration in place and time. E.g. we believe that the table that was in the room next door will still be there next time that we go into the room in the waking state but quite likely will not be if we are in a dream. Also, in the waking state, objects tend to remain the same, whereas in a dream a table might well change into a rhinoceros before our very dream eyes. Finally, the amount of control that we can exert over objects differs. E.g. we may be able to throw the dream table/rhinoceros into orbit or be unable to budge it at all whereas the waking table will usually behave in a predictable fashion.

We do not typically use the idea of matter at all when we identify an object as real or imaginary. Matter is simply a rationalization after the fact of the observed behavior and is not necessarily a useful concept. And, of course, we can never see matter; we only experience the various physical properties that we attribute to it.

And, if you think about it, why should matter exist? Just because we perceive round plates and windows does not mean that these things are partly made out of *roundness*; this is simply one of the properties that we discern. Similarly, the word "material" is used to describe a particular set of properties, such as solidity, shape, color, texture and so on. It is mere linguistic convenience to talk of something called matter that exhibits these sorts of properties.

Appearance and reality

Immanuel Kant, one of the most influential of all Western philosophers, made a clear differentiation between what we can know and
what we can never know. The former – the world of appearances
perceived through our senses – he called the *phenomenal* realm.
The latter – how things really are – he called the *noumenal.*

He observed that our senses are limited. We can only see a
narrow range of the electromagnetic spectrum for example and not
radio waves or X-rays. We can only hear part of the range of
sounds. We cannot smell with the sensitivity of a dog or navigate
like birds or salmon. We have no senses at all that can detect
magnetism or neutrinos for example. There are vast areas of
the universe that we can only be aware of indirectly through
instruments devised by science. If we do not have those instruments
or science has not yet devised them, those areas of the universe
simply do not exist for us. Even in those areas in which our senses
do operate, what they tell us is translated by organs and brain into
something totally alien to the "thing in itself" as he called the
reality of an object. Sensory impressions can only be like other
sensory impressions. They exist in the mind of the perceiver while
the reality exists outside and essentially independent of experience.
The noumenal is thus "transcendental" – hence the name given to
his variety of metaphysics: "transcendental Idealism." It is our
minds that impose form upon the raw data of perception.

One consequence of this is that any explanation for the
phenomenal world would have to lie outside of it and is therefore
effectively unknowable. We can never know whether God exists;
we are obliged to rely upon faith. In fact, Kant inferred that there
must be a God in order to reward us in the next life for virtuous

behavior in this one, since it was evident that immoral men often seemed to thrive in this life. If anyone expressed such a view now, we would think he was being ironic!

Furthermore, the concepts that we use to make sense of the world are just that – ideas in the mind – they have nothing to do with the way things really are. This applies even to those most fundamental concepts of all: space, time and causality.

Arthur Schopenhauer, continuing the line of thought initiated by Kant, suggested that the noumenal realm of "things in themselves" could not in fact consist of plural things. One thing must be separate from another thing, either in time or in space, in order for us to be aware of two things. If there were not this separation, we would only be aware of *one* thing. Accordingly, since time and space do not exist in reality, number cannot have any relevance. In fact, since causality is also just our way of explaining happenings in the world of appearances, the noumenal could not in any sense *cause* the phenomenal.

The phenomenal world must just be another way of looking at the noumenal. Everything that we see is simply a manifestation of this undifferentiated reality, including ourselves of course. There can be no such thing therefore as meaning or purpose, whether of our own lives or of the universe. In a sense, it is all an illusion. There is much in common with a number of eastern religions here, including some branches of Buddhism, Hinduism, Taoism, Sufism etc. and Schopenhauer did in fact have some exposure to these, though supposedly after he had developed his own understanding. But these ideas are not mystical or even abstruse. If you just think through how things are in your own experience, you are drawn inescapably to the same conclusions.

What do you see out of your window?

Practically speaking, then, what does all of this metaphysical speculation mean for our own experience? If you look out of your window into your garden, busy road or panoramic mountain vista (whatever it might be), what exactly do you see? Well, you might say, you see trees, flowers, cars, other houses and people etc. But is this really so? What is actually happening in the process of your seeing something outside of your window?

To begin with, there is light from the sun, moon or streetlight. But these are themselves things that you claim to see so let's ignore the source of the light for the moment. This light falls on the presumed objects and some of it is reflected back to your eyes. This reflected electromagnetic radiation passes through the pupil and impinges on various specialized receptors on the retina. This triggers electrical impulses that are sent along the optic nerve to the striate cortex – that part of the brain that has developed to process visual input. Neurotransmitter chemicals transfer the codified information across synapses and other parts of the brain are activated. This might involve memory units and motor activities to instruct muscles to move limbs to cause the body to avoid the possible breaking glass from the ball that has just been thrown at your window.

The precise mechanisms involved here are irrelevant and science is still unraveling them and trying to make sense of the detail. The point is that what we eventually see (and hear, feel, taste etc.) is never any actual *thing*, it is always only a mental construction of processes in the brain triggered by the electrical impulses sent by the sense organs.

Of course the brain is incredibly sophisticated in its operation and, as a result of this process, we are able to build up a detailed picture of a supposed separate world outside of our window. This is self-consistent most of the time. If we go out into the garden to look more closely at the ball that hit our window, we find we can actually pick it up and throw it back over the fence. It really does seem to be the one belonging to the dear little boy from next door.

Sometimes, however, we are deluded by our senses. There is, for example, one cleverly constructed room, into which you can look and see a person entering at one of the far corners and looking very small. As the person walks towards you, she appears to grow in size until she seems like a giant. It works by falsifying the perspective with a sloping floor. Your brain assumes that, since it looks like an ordinary room, it must *be* one. Even more extreme are the virtual reality simulators that are still in their infancy. One can imagine that, in the not too distant future, one will be able to strap electrodes and transmitters to various parts of the body and, in one's own living room, appear to visit exotic locations and indulge in even more exotic activities. And, if you are philosophically inclined, you might wonder about the distinction between reality and appearance. If precisely the same parts of the brain are stimulated, neuronic pathways traversed etc., in the VR environment as would be the case in the corresponding real environment, what exactly is the difference?

So this is the first point: namely that whatever may exist, separate from ourselves in a presumed external world, we are not directly aware of it. Nor can we ever be. We can only ever know of it indirectly through the medium of our senses and brain. These are what we might call "percepts", things that we *perceive* via our sensory equipment. What we perceive are not hard, distinct, separate objects but these percepts in our mind. In essence they are not really any different from thoughts and feelings which are similarly conceived and felt in our brain. We could group all of these together - percepts, thoughts or concepts, and feelings - and call them "mentations". These are events in the mental realm of the brain that represent themselves to our awareness as separate objects outside of our bodies or as images, words, pains etc. inside it.

No matter that we may think that there really is a world of objects and people separate from ourselves, there is simply no way that this could be proven since any supposed evidence or argument could only be presented in the same way. Words in a book arrive through the eyes, voices from other people arrive via the ears and so on. All eventually reaches the relevant part of the brain as pulses of electricity along nerves and movement of complex chemical molecules across synapses in the brain and it is only the results of these final stages that could be thought to be objectively known in any real sense. And, of course, in another sense, these activities are simply a part of the functioning of our body and thus not what we usually think of as separate at all. This is effectively what Berkeley was saying.

But what is actually outside your window?

In addition to the limited nature of our senses, all of the information that we receive via them takes time to reach our awareness. The movement of air sets up sympathetic vibrations of the eardrum which are transmitted in turn to the small bones of the inner ear. After further conversions and relaying, we become aware of the related brain activity that is sensed as sound. By the time that this occurs, the original trigger of the process may no longer be there. Similarly, the star that we think we see now may have exploded and dispersed throughout its galaxy thousands of years before its light reaches our eyes. Our senses always necessarily perceive only the past; we can never be aware of how things are this instant.

What we sense, and all that we can ever be aware of, is also dictated by the nature of our senses and the brain that processes the data. Even worse than this, we are conditioned to interpret the information according to learnt concepts in a way that is amenable to onward transmission by language.

Imagine that you are in a commercial fishing vessel; the nets have been drawn in and the contents emptied into the hold. With your handkerchief firmly clamped over your nose you venture down and examine the haul to see what size of fish has been caught. You quickly realize that they are all quite large fish, with nothing smaller than about four inches and, not being immediately very insightful, you conclude that this particular part of the sea is not inhabited by any small fish; perhaps the larger ones have eaten them all. Fortunately, before you make this observation known to the fishermen, you catch site of the net itself and realize that the holes in the net are about three inches square. The nets have filtered out anything smaller than that size so that we never see them in the catch.

And this is how it is with our mental apparatus. We have various modes, attitudes or concepts in our minds. We use these to analyze the data arriving from our senses in order to be able to interact with the world. Some of the modes will be genetic, selected by evolution because those members of our species that had them were better adapted for survival. The structure of our eyes would be an example of this, with the peripheral vision adapted to detect movement so that we might escape from predators.

Even such fundamental ideas as time, space and causation are only concepts that we use in order to try to make sense of this supposed external world. When we look out of our window we see what we describe as separate objects. These might be a greenhouse, a wheelbarrow, tree, dog and cat. We can differentiate the tree and the wheelbarrow because, we say, they occupy different locations in space.

We might look out of the window one minute and see the cat sitting in the wheel barrow. A few minutes later we might look out and see the dog in the same position. We do not conclude that the cat has somehow changed into a dog. We assume that they are distinct and separate and are merely occupying the same space but at a different time. We might even have reason to believe that the dog chased the cat away so that it could take its place in the barrow, providing an additional causal explanation for the transformation.

All of these concepts are our ways of making sense of the world. They are the nets through which we filter our perceptual data in order to come up with a usable map of our environment. It is inevitable that the world will seem to conform to our interpretation of it since we have no other source to use for comparison. Suppose that a pan-galactic, five dimensional alien with X-ray "vision" and magnetic "hearing" materializes and takes an inventory of the garden. If we subsequently compared notes, there would simply be no grounds for mutual understanding unless conceivably in some purely mathematical sense. This is effectively what Kant was saying.

Metaphors for reality and appearance

The most pervasive concepts that we use to differentiate objects in the world are the ones of name and form. Our eyes and hands are aware of shapes and, in order to be able to refer to them in their absence, we give them names. This is how we saw, in the example above, that the cat object in the garden outside of our window came to be replaced by a dog object. Probably the shapes and colors were so specific that we had given them even more specific names and were able to say that Bonzo was now sitting where Tiddles had been before.

But this way of dividing up the world into bits and giving each bit its own name is so ingrained in us that we never think to question what is happening. Suppose I take this gold ring off my finger (ok, I don't actually have one but you can use your imagination). I hand it to you and you can feel its shape, see its color and luster. Perhaps it is the wrong size to fit on your own finger but you would have no difficulty in confirming that it is, indeed, a ring. I now take the ring back and go into my workshop, from which I emerge a couple of hours later and hand you a thimble. Again you can see and feel it. It has those tiny indentations in the end for preventing it slipping when you push a needle through cloth. If I ask you what it is, you will no doubt confirm that it is a thimble.

Now, as you will have already guessed, what I did was to put the ring into the furnace in my workshop. I melted it down and poured the gold into a thimble cast. This is a simple enough transformation and nothing to cause our brains any dilemma. Or is it? What did we *really* have to begin with? If you claim that we really had a ring, I will dispute it. The ring no longer exists and, I will assert, never *really* existed in the first place. Similarly, I am saying that the thimble, which you now hold in your hand, does not *really* exist; it is just another transient name and form. The only real existent entity throughout the entire process is the gold. The gold existed before the ring was made, while it was in the form of a ring, after I had melted it down and it still exists now that I have formed it into the shape of a thimble.

Here, you will see that I am choosing to use the word "real" in a very precise way, similar to that used by Parmenides. It is somewhat at odds with the way in which we normally, and carelessly, use it. I want it to mean permanent, eternal, unchanging; specifically it exists in all three periods of time, past, present and future. We could ask a goldsmith to work it into unending and intricate shapes and forms to serve different purposes, whether as a precision part in a delicate mechanism or as a piece of jewelry to adorn some bodily part of a loved one. But no matter what arbitrary form it happens to take and irrespective of what we choose to call it and in what language, it will remain what it always was *in reality* – gold.

I will return to this metaphor later but what I would like you to agree to conclude at the moment is that our way of thinking and the language that we use forces us to see the world in certain ways. Given that we can never see it as it actually is, this must mean that we are more than likely to be mistaken in our understanding. Providing that our mental picture allows us to function, find food, avoid predators, reproduce and so on, we will continue as an animal species. Indeed, it has clearly been very efficient in this respect, since we seem to be gradually eliminating all other species from the planet, but this does not mean that our way of seeing and interpreting the world is correct. All it means is that it has been successful in evolutionary terms, at least in the tiny span of time that mankind has been around.

In one sense, language itself could be seen as the root of our problems. There is good reason to suppose that a baby does not see the seeming objects in the world as separate from himself. There is simply an amorphous, undifferentiated mass of data impinging on his senses, sometimes associated with pleasurable feelings, sometimes not. But there is initially no reason to suppose that a sensation of redness or a sound should be considered to be indicative of something separate from oneself any more than is a feeling of discomfort or pain.

But all too soon, a parent is pointing and naming: "look, this is a ball; you 'Peter', me 'Mummy'". From that moment on, it is downhill all the way. The world is divided up into objects, some desirable and others feared. Our entire outlook on life is dictated by the language we use to think about reality and communicate our thoughts with "others."

In respect of the gold ring just discussed, we should actually refer to it as "ringy gold". Our habit of switching the object and attribute is a tremendous source of confusion. It is not "a ring made of gold at all" but gold that just happens to be in the form of a ring... for the moment. Even gold is only a particular and temporary configuration of protons, neutrons and electrons, so that it too is really an adjective or attribute. Similarly, protons etc. are themselves made up of still smaller particles, called quarks. Ultimately, everything is only name and form of that fundamental reality which is changeless – the only noun which is not an attribute of something else.

Another metaphor that is helpful to enable us to understand how we can be so wrong in our understanding of ourselves and the world is very famous in Eastern philosophy. It is usually referred to simply as the "rope and snake" metaphor. Suppose that you are walking along late at night in the jungle when, coiled up on the path ahead, you see a snake. In fact, when you get the torch out of your rucksack and direct it towards the snake, you see that it is only a rope that your tour guide had put there to frighten you. It is perfectly understandable that your imagination would be somewhat heightened in these circumstances but the fact remains that you have made a mistake. What you actually saw was a rope. There is no denying the fact; it is there, complete with fraying end in the beam of your torch. Equally certain is that just a moment ago you were convinced that it was a snake and nothing would have induced you to move any further forwards on the path (except perhaps for a tiger approaching from the other direction).

So what is actually happening in this example? The rope is real; the snake was an illusion, an image taken from memory and superimposed upon the rope. It was the darkness of the night that obscured the true form of the rope and our minds projected the unreality of the snake. Another way of looking at the situation is that, when we made the initial observation we thought "there is a snake." It was certainly true that there was something there so that the "there is" part of our thought was true. What was false was the "a snake" part of the sentence. Despite the fact that there was not really a snake there, we behaved in exactly the same way as if there had been. Adrenaline was pumped into the bloodstream, we became afraid and ran away, probably wondering whether it was poisonous or not and whether there was an antidote if we were bitten.

The reason for all of this analysis and the purpose of the

metaphor itself is to suggest that we make the same kind of mistake whenever we look out at the world or, indeed, make an observation of any kind relating to what we think of as reality. When we look out of our window, it is certainly true that there seems to be something out there but what is it? Whenever we do this, we immediately search in our memory for something that we can latch on to and give a name or names for what we see. Look, there are a tree and a wheelbarrow with a cat in it (or is it a dog?). Perhaps *in reality* it is none of these things. After all, we have already acknowledged above (hopefully) that we can never actually perceive reality since we will always be limited by the nature of our senses, our concepts and our language.

Similarly, when we say "I am a man (or woman)", it is certainly true that "I am" – this is the one thing of which we can always be certain, that we exist. But perhaps the "man (or woman)" part of this statement is false, a concept that we habitually superimpose upon the reality just as we superimposed the snake idea upon the reality of the rope. We attribute all sorts of properties to our world. It is cold and inhospitable or friendly and exciting. Perhaps the assigning of these characteristics is no different from describing the snake as fast-moving and venomous. When the snake is really a rope, these adjectives are clearly inappropriate. We have already said that the way in which we see the world is also erroneous; a partial and biased picture governed by the nature of our senses and mind. This being the case, much if not all of the way that we describe the world may be incorrect.

I can almost hear you saying now that, yes, this is all very interesting but there is one major difference. In the case of the snake, all I have to do is bring along a torch and immediately the illusion is dispelled. I can see that it is really a rope and all of the problems are seen to have been imaginary. When you suggest that the same might apply to our perception of the universe, nothing at all happens. I still see my dog sitting in the wheelbarrow outside my window. But, in fact, the analogy does still hold if you think about it. In the case of the snake, if I simply *tell* you that it is really only a rope but you do not actually see this for yourself in the beam of the torch, it is very likely that you will not believe me. After all, the risk of making a mistake could be the loss of your life. Similarly, you could say that you have invested everything in your present belief in the reality of your world. All of your purpose and meaning derives from its being real and, in a sense, your life as you know it might fall apart if it were suddenly known for a fact that you are mistaken.

What is needed to convince you is to shine the light of knowledge onto the situation. You have to listen, read, reflect and meditate etc. on all of this information and more, until you come to recognize the truth. You have to be convinced that an acceptance of this will not be the dreadful end that you might now think it would be, but on the contrary, only an end to misery, lack of purpose, worry etc. Although you are unlikely to acknowledge it yet, your whole life has had as its ultimate purpose a search for your true nature. Once found, it is as though previously blind you are now able to see for the first time the true nature of your self and reality in all its glory.

Imagine that you are walking in a hot desert. All you can see for miles around is sand, and you are very thirsty. Suddenly, through the heat haze in the distance, you see a lake surrounded by palm trees and you groan with relief at the thought of the water soon to slake your thirst. But then your weary brain cuts in with the memory that that this sort of thing has been reported before; that in all probability it is only a mirage. You begin to panic but then you hear a voice in your head, telling you not to get excited. If you make the effort to remember, it says, you will recall that you are not actually walking anywhere; that you are in fact testing out the very latest in virtual reality simulation and isn't it incredibly realistic? The terror disappears immediately and you begin to look around with curiosity to see if you can discover any anomalies in this manufactured world. Then you wake up and realize the whole thing was a dream.

At each successive stage in the above example, your mental outlook undergoes a complete paradigm shift. The basis from which you had formed judgments about the world in front of you underwent a radical transformation. What you had previously thought to be real was now known to be unreal and you had a new set of criteria for making judgments. This mechanism by which one view or assessment of a situation is contradicted by a new experience is called 'sublation." Thus it is being proposed that the way in which we currently see and interpret the world and ourselves is a mistake and that it is possible to acquire new knowledge that will sublate our current beliefs. This concept also provides another way in which we can define what we mean by "reality": reality is that which cannot be sublated by another experience.

This is similar to what was said about name and form. Reality is that which does not change; it was the same in the past as it is now and as it will be in the future, just like the gold in the metaphor. In the past the gold might have been embedded in a nugget in a stream in the Klondike. Someone found the nugget, extracted the gold and fashioned a ring out of it. If you don't particularly like the form in which it is now, you can have it melted down again and made into a thimble. Throughout past, present and future it remains as gold; this is its reality. Its form has changed radically and we have names for these various forms that define its particular appearance at any given point in time. But these names and forms are only the way that we currently see and interpret what we see. We should not make the mistake of assuming that we *really* have a ring in front of us now. This particular appearance is only transient.

In the same way, you and I, the cat, dog and wheelbarrow are only transient names and forms and should not be mistaken for the true reality, which of course you do not yet know and cannot know objectively. I *exist*. This is reality, it cannot be denied. But we cannot say this of the world. Certainly there is something, we cannot deny it since we can see it, but all that we can say of it is that it is "not non-existent." All that we can know for certain, *in an objective sense*, is that it is not the names and forms that we habitually but mistakenly impose upon it.

Who are we then?

Finally, although I am taking the risk that you really will throw the book out of the window (to see if you can hit the dog), I would like to take this discussion to its ultimate conclusion so as not to waste the impetus of the argument.

I began the chapter by explaining how we can only ever be aware of what is in our minds, whether these are perceptions, thoughts or feelings. We can only ever *infer* the existence of separate objects external to our mind on the basis of our perceptions. This is the position of Idealism, as put forward by Berkeley. In fact, he did not really follow through the force of his own arguments and believed that objects *did* actually exist. He said that, if we go out of a room in which we have observed a table and chair, those items still continue to exist, even though we can no longer see them *because God can still see them.*

Of course, this could never carry any weight with atheistic listeners and, more to the point, simply does not go far enough. What Berkeley did not admit, at least publicly, is that the perceptions themselves, together with thoughts and feelings can all be regarded as objects. Although he had argued that we can never be directly aware of actual objects (if they exist), perceptions too are effectively quasi objects. All mentations are subtle objects in that we, as subject, are aware of them.

This begs the next question – who are we, the subject? Whoever we are is conscious of the body as something separate. And, lest we jump to the conclusion that we are the mind, this has to be regarded in exactly the same way. Whatever occurs in the mind, we are conscious of it as something separate and therefore we cannot be it.

The ultimate conclusion has to be that all of these so-called things are arising in consciousness. If they were not, we could not be aware of them. In order for something to *exist*, we have to be aware of it, by definition. The word "exist" means to have "objective reality" and, clearly, this requires a subject. It is simply not meaningful to suppose that anything could exist outside of consciousness. What could that mean? Such "things" as unicorns or balrogs exist in the sense that they are things that we imagine – they are concepts or dreams. As soon as we imagine something, that becomes a subtle object.

You might argue that some things in the past were outside of consciousness but are not now: say the HIV virus for example. A hundred years ago, no one could even conceive of something that could behave in the way that this does and wreak such havoc. But time itself is simply another concept, appearing in consciousness just like any other. It is just not possible to conceive of anything that is not an appearance in consciousness. As soon as we conceive it, it exists as a conception. Bodies are appearances; diseases are appearances along with their symptoms, pains, epidemiology and cures. Death is an appearance, as is history. History is only a set of ideas and data now presented to a conscious mind studying such information.

And think of this: whether or not you care to accept any of these arguments, in order to be aware (or unaware) of anything or any concept at all, there must first be consciousness. This is impossible to deny.

There is nothing, can be nothing that is not an appearance in consciousness. And here I do not mean something outside, appearing *to* consciousness; I mean appearing *in* consciousness. And now it is but a short step to say that the appearances in consciousness are simply name and form being imposed upon the substratum. They are the ring or the thimble being imposed upon the gold. In the final analysis, there simply is nothing other than consciousness. Consciousness is all there is. And I do not mean consciousness as a concept for that would require a conceiver and the whole thing would lead to an infinite regression. In order to speak of it at all, we have to call "it" something, even though it isn't any "thing." Call it consciousness, absolute, God or what you will. There are not two things. To return to Kant's differentiation into phenomenal and noumenal, consciousness is not a phenomenon – it is the noumenal.

This also means, of course, that we can say something more about the so-called world. It was stated earlier that we cannot say anything in an objective sense other than that it is not the names and forms. But we can now say something subjectively – the world is not other than my self.

Another metaphor that can help in thinking about this is that of the Mt. Rushmore sculptures that was mentioned earlier. We are so intent upon looking at the carved faces that we fail to see that they are all made out of a single rock. Similarly, we go through our entire lives, seeing and interacting with supposed objects and people, not realizing that in reality they and we are one un-differentiated consciousness. There is only the rock itself contemplating the form of the sculptures.

So there you have it! You are probably sitting there with mouth metaphorically (or even literally) wide open in disbelief. But before I move on to the final summary, I would just like to emphasize how important the above is in terms of our search. If we are living our lives in the hope of acquiring material possessions, achieving important positions in our employment or society, meeting famous or beautiful people, writing best-selling books on the meaning of life or anything else that is dependent upon the world being as we have always thought it to be – having a real existence and containing "things" and "people" – then we need to be very sure that we are not making a terrible mistake. We would feel very silly if, at the end of our lives, we discovered that we had expended all of our energies avoiding or fighting an assumed snake that turned out to be only a rope.

Conclusion - We *are* happiness

Now the picture is complete and the logic leading to those single word answers that I promised you at the beginning of the book is inescapable.

Firstly, we can acknowledge that the only times when we are really happy are when we "forget ourselves." This might be in the moment of fulfilling some long-term desire (so that we are temporarily desire-less) or when feeling our way along a ledge above a precipice, with attention fully focused. It is only so long as we delude ourselves that we are a body, mind, intellect or soul that we find ourselves in misery and without a sense of meaning or purpose. The ego is an illusion and it has to disappear before the underlying happiness is revealed.

Secondly, there is never any question in our minds that we exist but we habitually identify ourselves with something that we are not and this action takes us away from our true nature and hence from happiness. We are continually looking outside of ourselves for meaning, purpose and happiness when these can never be found outside.

Thirdly, when we analyze our experience, it is found that everything that we see, feel or think is nothing more than an appearance in mind. We can never assign any reality to any "thing", gross or subtle, independently of these appearances. Furthermore, since they are appearing *to* me, I cannot *be* any of those things. All things, including the mind itself and the illusory ego, are simply appearances. They appear to whatever it is that we truly are which, for the sake of a meaningful name, has been called "Consciousness."

Fourthly, it would not be meaningful to talk about Consciousness being happy or unhappy. Being complete and without limitations of any sort, it is more appropriate to say that Consciousness *is* happiness. This, then, is an aspect of my true nature. Since I am Consciousness, there is nothing that I need, nothing to be achieved, nowhere to which I have to get. I am already perfect and complete – I *am* happiness.

All phenomena – whether supposed external objects, including other people, feelings of joy or pain, thoughts, spiritual or profane – are appearances within Consciousness. They arise within Consciousness, stay around for a time and then subside back into Consciousness. Ultimately they are nothing other than Consciousness, just as the rock-face sculptures are nothing more than the rock out of which they were carved. I could, of course, equally well say that they arise within *me*, abide and return to *me*. How could any of these ever-changing, transient phenomena "matter" to me in any sense of that word? Everything is perfect, from the delicacy of the most exquisite orchid to the mushroom cloud over Hiroshima. Nothing is special or privileged in any way – all is simply Consciousness. The idea that something matters is itself just another appearance in Consciousness. All appearances are nothing other than Consciousness, which is all there is. I am that Consciousness.

So, there you have it. There is no ego; there is no person; you are not the body, mind or intellect; there is no individual soul to survive death or to reincarnate. You cannot choose to act and, in any case, *you* do nothing at all. Mars does not exist. There is no point in worrying about what you ought to do or what the purpose of life might be. You, as an individual, do not exist. All of your concerns derive from a mistaken sense of identification. You are not any thing. You are everything. You cannot become something else; there is nothing that you are not already.

There is nothing lacking – we have no limitations. Accordingly, there is nothing to desire. The purpose of life, to the extent that this has any meaning, is simply to realize this truth. There is nothing to be done, nowhere to go. Ambitions and purpose are irrelevant – we have everything already. That which is already infinite, perfect and complete cannot become anything – change simply has no meaning. Until this realization becomes absolute, all that you can do is to reflect upon all of this, allow the understanding to grow until the time comes when the ignorance finally falls away and you become established in this truth. You are not yourself, you are *the* Self (or Absolute, or God). And That is all there is.

The answers to those two questions in the introduction now follow automatically, though as you will now realize this can only be appreciated *after* you have read the book! (This is a warning for those of you who are cheating and referring to the end after reading the opening section of the book.)

Q: "Who am I?"
A: Everything.

Q: "What really matters?"
A: Nothing.

Bibliography

Western philosophy

1. *Think. A Compelling Introduction to Philosophy.* Simon Blackburn. Oxford University Press, 1999. ISBN 0-19-210024-6.

2. *Confessions of a Philosopher.* Bryan Magee. Weidenfeld & Nicholson, 1997. ISBN 0-297-81959-3.

3. *Three Philosophical Moralists.* George C. Kerner. Clarendon Press, 1990. ISBN 0-19-824227-1.

4. *An Introduction to Philosophical Analysis.* John Howpers. Routledge, 1997. ISBN 0-415-15793-5.

5. *History of Western Philosophy.* Bertrand Russell. Routledge, 1991. ISBN 0-415-07854-7.

6. *Thinking Philosophically.* Richard E. Creel. Blackwell, 2001. ISBN 0-631-21935-8.

7. *The Oxford Companion to Philosophy.* Ed. Ted Honderich. Oxford University Press, 1995. ISBN 0-19-866132-0.

8. *The Western Philosophers.* E. W. F. Tomlin. Hutchinson, 1968. ISBN 09-086801-3.

9. *Philosophy Made Simple.* Richard H. Popkin & Avrum Stroll. Doubleday, 1969. ISBN 0491-00789-2.

10. *Fifty Major Philosophers.* Diané Collinson. Routledge, 1988. ISBN 0-415-03135-4.

11. *A History of the Mind.* Nicholas Humphrey. Vintage Books, 1993. ISBN 0-09-922311-2.

12. *Fifty Key Contemporary Thinkers.* John Lechte. Routledge, 1994. ISBN 0-415-07408-8.

13. *Ludwig Wittgenstein.* Ray Monk. Vintage, 1991.

ISBN 0-09-988370-8.

14. *Plato not Prozac*. Lou Marinoff. First Quill, 2000.
    ISBN 0-06-019328-X.

15. *On The Meaning Of Life*. John Cottingham. Routledge,
    2003. ISBN 0-415-24800-0.

16. Website: Philosophy Pages from Garth Kemerling.
    Comprehensive survey with history, timeline, dictionary
    etc. (http://www.philosophypages.com/)

17. The Internet Encyclopedia of Philosophy: A comprehensive
    set of articles by experts on many aspects of Western
    Philosophy. (http://www.utm.edu/research/iep/)

18. The "Need to Know" and the Meaning of Life. Kelley L.
    Ross, Ph.D. (http://www.friesian.com/#contents).

19. *The Mysterious Flame. Conscious minds in a material
    world*. Colin McGinn. Basic Books, 1999. ISBN 0-0465-
    01422-4

20. *The Questions of Life*. Fernando Savater. Polity Press, 2002.
    ISBN 0-7456-2629-7.

Sociology, psychology and other

21. *Into the Silent Land*. Paul Broks. Atlantic Books, 2003.
    ISBN 1-903809-55-X.

22. *How the Mind Works*. Steven Pinker. Penguin Books, 1998.
    ISBN 0-14-024491-3.

23. *The Wisdom of Insecurity. A Message for an Age of Anxiety*.
    Alan Watts. Rider, 1994. ISBN 0-7126-9588-5.

24. *Mechanism of Mind*. Edward de Bono. Viking, 1969.
    ISBN 0-140-21445-3.

25. *The Farther Reaches of Human Nature*. Abraham Maslow.

Viking, 1971. ISBN 0-140-21645-6.

26. *The Man Who Mistook His Wife for a Hat*. Oliver Sacks. Picador, 1986. ISBN 0-330-29491-1.

27. *Flow: The Psychology of Happiness*. Mihaly Csikszentmihalyi. Rider, 1992. ISBN 0-7126-5477-1.

28. *The Language Instinct*. Steven Pinker. Penguin, 1995. ISBN 0-14-017529-6.

29. *The Purpose of Life*. Donald Cameron. Woodhill, 2001. ISBN 0-9540291-0-0.

30. *Meanings of Life*. Roy F. Baumeister. The Guilford Press, 1991. ISBN 0-89862-531-9.

31. *Man's Search for Meaning*. Viktor E. Frankl. Beacon Press, 2000. ISBN 0-807-01426-5.

32. *Does Life Have a Meaning?* Milton K. Munitz. Prometheus Books, 1993. ISBN 0-87975-860-0.

33. *A Guide for the Perplexed*. E. F. Schumacher. Abacus, 1977. ISBN 0-349-13130-9.

34. *The Wrong Side of the Edge*. Ron Watters, Idaho State University. Paper downloaded from Internet.

35. *The Quest for Excitement and the Safe Society*. Gunnar Breivik, Norwegian University of Sport and Physical Education, Oslo. Paper downloaded from Internet.

36. *Not-so Total Recall*. John McCrone. New Scientist 13th May 2003.

37. *The Pursuit of Happiness*. Michael Bond. New Scientist 4th Oct 2003.

38. *The Pleasure Seekers*. Helen Phillips. New Scientist 11th Oct 2003.

39. Life *Satisfaction: The State Of Knowledge And Implications*

For Government. UK Government Strategy Unit. Nick Donovan and David Halpern. December 2002.

40. *Feeling Good About Fredrickson's Positive Emotions*. David G. Myers. *Prevention & Treatment*, Volume 3, Article 2, posted March 7, 2000

41. Psychology (6th Edition Study Guide). David G. Myers and Richard Straub. Worth Publishing; 6th edition (July 2000). ISBN 1572599588.

42. The Pursuit of Happiness. Who is happy – and why? David G. Myers. The Aquarian Press, 1993. ISBN 1 85538 273 3.

43. Wanting More in an Age of Plenty. David G. Myers. (Article adapted from *The American Paradox: Spiritual Hunger in an Age of Plenty* by David G. Myers, Yale University Press, 2000) (http://www.christianitytoday.com).

44. Wealth, Well-Being and the New American Dream. David G. Myers, April 2000. (http://www.newdream.org/).

45. The Psychology of Happiness. Michael Argyle. Routledge, Second Edition, 2001. ISBN 0-415-22665-1.

Advaita philosophy

46. *The Book of One*. Dennis Waite. O Books, 2003. ISBN 1-903816-41-6.

47. *Consciousness in Advaita Vedanta*. William M. Indich. Motilal Banarsidass Publishers, Delhi 1995. ISBN 81-208-1251-9.

48. *Advaita Vedanta – A Philosophical Reconstruction*. Eliot Deutsch. University of Hawaii Press, Honolulu 1973. ISBN 0-8248-0271-3.

49. *The Chandogya Upanishad*. Commentary by Swami

Krishnananda. The Divine Life Society, Himalyas, India 1984. No ISBN.

50. *The Mandukya Upanishad with Gaudapada's Karika and Shankara's Commentary*. Translated by Swami Nikhilananda. Advaita Ashrama, Himalayas, India 1987. No ISBN.

51. *The Ten Principal Upanishads*. Put into English by Shree Purohit Swami and W. B. Yeats. Faber and Faber Limited, London 1970. ISBN 0-571-09363-9.

52. *The Self and its States*. Andrew O. Fort. Motilal Banarsidass Publishers Pvt. Ltd., Delhi 1990. ISBN 81-208-0633-6.

53. *The Brihadaranyaka Upanishad*. Swami Krishnananda. The Divine Life Trust Society 1984. No ISBN.

54. *Discourses on Mandukya Upanishad*. Swami Chinmayananda. Central Chinmaya Mission Trust, Bombay, 1990. No ISBN.

55. *Four Upanishads*. Swami Paramananda. Sri Ramakrishna Math, Madras, 1974. ISBN 81-7120-233-0.

56. *The Bhagavad Gita, with the Commentary of Sri Shankaracharya*. Samata Books, Madras, 1977. No ISBN.

57. *The Holy Geeta: Commentary by Swami Chinmayananda*. Central Chinmaya Mission Trust, 1996. No ISBN.

58. *The Bhagavad Gita: Commentary by Swami Chidbhavananda*. Sri Ramakrishna Tapovanam, 1986. No ISBN.

59. *Astavakra Samhita: Translation and Commentary by Swami Nityaswarupananda*. Advaita Ashrama, 1990. No ISBN.

60. *Astavakra Gita: Commentary by Swami Chinmayananda*. Central Chinmaya Mission Trust, 1997. No ISBN.

61. *Pancadasi of Sri Vidyaranya Swami*. English Translation by Swami Swahananda. Sri Ramakrishna Math, Madras, 1980. No ISBN.

62. *Sri Shankaracharya's Bhaja Govindam*. Swami Chinmayananda. Central Chinmaya Mission Trust, 1991. No ISBN.

63. *Atmabodha, Knowledge of Self*. Commentary by A. Parthasarathy. Vedanta Life Institute, Bombay, 1990. No ISBN.

64. *Shankara's Crest-Jewel of Discrimination (Vivekachudamani)*. Translated by Swami Prabhavananda and Christopher Isherwood. Vedanta Press, 1978. ISBN 0-87481-038-8.

65. *Introduction to Vedanta. Understanding the Fundamental Problem*. Swami Dayananda. Vision Books, New Delhi, 1989. ISBN 81-7094-037-0.

66. *Vedanta Treatise. A. Parthasarathy*. Vedanta Life Institute, Bombay, 1992. No ISBN.

67. *Brahma Sutra bhashya of Shankaracharya*. Translated by Swami Gambhirananda. Advaita Ashrama, 1996. ISBN 81-7505-105-1.

68. *The Gospel of Sri Ramakrishna, Abridged Edition*. Translated into English with an Introduction by Swami Nikhilananda. Ramakrishna-Vivekananda Center, 1958. ISBN 0-911206-02-7.

69. *The Essential Teachings of Hinduism*. Edited by Kerry Brown. Arrow Books Limited, London, 1990. ISBN 0-09-978530-7.

70. *Talks with Sri Ramana Maharshi*. Sri Ramanashramam,

Tiruvannamalai, 1994. No ISBN.

71. *Maha Yoga of Bhagavan Sri Ramana*. "Who". Sri
    Ramanashramam, Tiruvannamalai, 1984. No ISBN.

72. *I am That*. Sri Nisargadatta Maharaj. Chetana (P) Ltd.,
    Bombay, 1981. ISBN 085655-406-5.

73. *Pointers From Nisargadatta Maharaj*. Ramesh S. Balsekar.
    Chetana (P) Ltd., Bombay, 1982. ISBN 81-85300-19-4.

74. *Acceptance of What Is – a Book About Nothing*. Wayne
    Liquorman. Advaita Fellowship, 2000. ISBN 0-929448-19-7.

75. *Seeds for the Soul*. Chuck Hillig. Trafford Publishing, 2003.
    ISBN 1-55395-844-6.

76. *Be Who You Are*. Jean Klein. Element, 1989.
    ISBN 1-85230-103-1.

77. *I Am*. Jean Klein. Third Millennium Publications, 1989.
    ISBN 1-877769-19-3.

78. *The Truth Is*. Sri H. W. L. Poonja. Yudhishtara, 1995. No ISBN.

79. *The Open Secret*. Tony Parsons. The Connections, 1995.
    ISBN 0-9533032-0-9.

80. *The Yoga Sutras of Patanjali*. Translation and Commentary
    by Sri Swami Satchidananada. Integral Yoga Publications,
    1990. ISBN 0-932040-38-1.

81. *Vedanta Sutras of Narayana Guru*. Swami Muni Narayana
    Prasad. D. K. Printworld (P) Ltd., New Delhi, 1997.
    ISBN 81-246-0085-6.

82. *The Science of Enlightenment*. Nitin Trasi. D. K. Printworld
    (P) Ltd., New Delhi, 1997. ISBN 81-246-0130-5.

83. *Eternity Now. Dialogues on Awareness*. Francis Lucille.
    Truespeech Productions, 1996. No ISBN.

84. *Clarity*. Nathan Gill. GOB Publications, 2000. No ISBN.

85. Self Enquiry. Tri-Annual Review of the Ramana Maharshi Foundation, U.K. ISSN 1357-0935.

86. *The Book. On the Taboo Against Knowing Who You Are.* Alan Watts. Vintage Books, 1966. ISBN 0-679-72300-5.

87. *What is Meditation?* Osho. Element, 1995. ISBN 1-85230-726-9.

88. *I Am That.* Discourses on the Isa Upanishad. Bhagwan Shree Rajneesh. Rajneesh Foundation International, 1984. ISBN 0-88050-580-X.

89. *Heartbeat of the Absolute.* Commentaries on the Ishavasya Upanishad. Osho. Element, 1980. ISBN 1-85230-490-1.

90. *The Mustard Seed. Discourses on the Sayings of Jesus from the Gospel According to Thomas.* Osho. Element, 1975. ISBN 1-85230-498-7.

91. *The Penguin Krishnamurti Reader.* Edited by Mary Lutyens. Penguin Books Ltd., 1954, 1963, 1964. No ISBN.

92. *Atmananda Tattwa Samhita. The Direct Approach to Truth as Expounded by Sri Atmananda.* Compiled by K. Padmanabha Menon. Advaita Publishers, 1973. No ISBN.

93. *DR^ig-dR^ishya-viveka. An inquiry into the nature of the seer and the seen.* With Commentary by Swami Nikhilananda. Sri Ramakrishna Ashrama, Mysore, 1976. ISBN 0-902-47927-X.

94. *Kena Upanishad. Swami Muni Narayana Prasad.* D. K. Printworld (P) Ltd., New Delhi 1995. ISBN 81-246-0034-1.

95. *Dispelling Illusion, Gaudapada's Alatashanti.* Translated and Introduction Douglas A. Fox. State University of New York Press, 1993. ISBN 0-7914-1502-3.

96. *The Teaching of the Bhagavad Gita. Swami Dayananda.*

Vision Books Pvt. Ltd., 1989. ISBN 81-7094-032-X.

97. *Atma Darshan (At the Ultimate)*. Sri Atmananda (Krishnamenon). Advaita Publishers, 1989. ISBN 0-914793-16-0.

98. *Atma Nirvritti (Freedom and Felicity in the Self)*. Sri Atmananda (Krishnamenon). Advaita Publishers, 1989. ISBN 0-914793-05-5.

99. *Chandogya Upanishad*. Swami Swahananda. Sri Ramakrishna Math, Madras, 1980. No ISBN.

100. *Sayings of Sri Ramakrishna – An Exhaustive Collection*. Sri Ramakrishna Math, Madras, 1987. No ISBN.

101. *No Mind I am the Self*. David Godman. Bhanumathy Ramanadham Sri Rakshmana Ashram. No ISBN. (Out of Print)

102. Upadesha Sahasri. Sri Shankaracharya. Sri Ramakrishna Math, Mylapore, Madras, 1989. ISBN 81-7120-059-1.

103. *Be As You Are. The Teachings of Sri Ramana Maharshi*. Edited by David Godman. Arkana, 1985. ISBN 0-14-019062-7.

104. Notes on Spiritual Discourse of Shri Atmananda taken by Nitya Tripta. Manuscript copy of Proposed second edition down loaded from www.advaita.org.uk.

105. *Awakening to the Dream. The gift of lucid living*. Leo Hartong. Trafford, 2001. ISBN 1-4120-0425-X.

106. *Doing Nothing. Coming to the end of the spiritual search*. Steven Harrison. Jeremy P. Tarcher/Putnam, 2002. ISBN 1-58542-172-3.

107. *The Power of Now. A guide to spiritual enlightenment*. Eckhart Tolle. Hodder & Stoughton, 1999. ISBN 0 340 733500.

Index

O

is a symbol of the world,
of oneness and unity. O Books
explores the many paths of wholeness
and spiritual understanding which
different traditions have developed down
the ages. It aims to bring this knowledge
in accessible form, to a general readership,
providing practical spirituality to today's seekers.

For the full list of over 200 titles covering:

- CHILDREN'S PRAYER, NOVELTY AND GIFT BOOKS
- CHILDREN'S CHRISTIAN AND SPIRITUALITY
- CHRISTMAS AND EASTER
- RELIGION/PHILOSOPHY
- SCHOOL TITLES
- ANGELS/CHANNELLING
- HEALING/MEDITATION
- SELF-HELP/RELATIONSHIPS
- ASTROLOGY/NUMEROLOGY
- SPIRITUAL ENQUIRY
- CHRISTIANITY, EVANGELICAL
  AND LIBERAL/RADICAL
- CURRENT AFFAIRS
- HISTORY/BIOGRAPHY
- INSPIRATIONAL/DEVOTIONAL
- WORLD RELIGIONS/INTERFAITH
- BIOGRAPHY AND FICTION
- BIBLE AND REFERENCE
- SCIENCE/PSYCHOLOGY

Please visit our website,
www.O-books.net

David
Jim McCoughlan
Pulizet peizer
John Adams Book

Lettr to (Sara)
?
_____

Look 4 the Books